The Belles-Lettres Series

SECTION III
THE ENGLISH DRAMA

FROM ITS BEGINNING TO THE PRESENT DAY

GENERAL EDITOR
GEORGE PIERCE BAKER

PROFESSOR OF DRAMATIC LITERATURE
IN HARVARD UNIVERSITY

NEWES
From Perin in Cornwall:
OF
A most Bloody and vn-exampled Murther

very lately committed by a Father on his owne
Sonne *(who was lately returned from the Indyes)* at
the Inſtigation of a mercileſſe
Step-mother.

*Together with their ſeuerall moſt wretched endes, being
all performed in the Month of Septem-
ber laſt.* Anno. 1618.

LONDON
Printed by E. A. and are to be ſolde at *Chriſt-Church* gate. 1618.

THE
LONDON MERCHANT

OR

THE HISTORY OF GEORGE BARNWELL

AND

FATAL CURIOSITY

By GEORGE LILLO

EDITED BY

ADOLPHUS WILLIAM WARD, Litt.D., F.B.A.

MASTER OF PETERHOUSE COLLEGE
CAMBRIDGE, ENGLAND

BOSTON, U.S.A., AND LONDON
D. C. HEATH & CO., PUBLISHERS

Biography

VERY little is known concerning the personal life of
George Lillo, the author of the two plays which are reprinted in this volume, and each of which may be said to
have a place of its own in the history of the modern
drama. His name is Flemish, and he was very probably
a descendant of refugees whom religious persecution had
driven to this country. ‘Lillo’ was the name of the fort
that stood above Antwerp on the northern bank of the
Scheldt.[1]

On the occasion of the marriage, in 1734, of the Prin-
cess Royal of Great Britain (Anne, daughter of King
George II) to the Prince of Orange (William IV),
Lillo produced a masque entitled *Britannia and Batavia*.
In this quite unpretending and uninteresting production,
its two eponymous personages are introduced as the joint
defenders of freedom against Spain and Rome, and it is
proclaimed as Britannia's duty to requite Batavia, by means
of the match now concluded, for the services of her
champion Liberto (William III).[2] Other passages in
Lillo's writings indicate his probably inherited hatred of

[1] I am reminded of this circumstance by Mr. G. Edmundson, one of our
foremost living authorities on the history and literature of the Netherlands.
He adds: ‘ Motley speaks of the beautiful country house and farm of
Lillo. The name was probably that of the owner, and it is quite possible
that a family of that name may have been among the refugees who came
to England, after the capture of Antwerp by Parma.’

[2] Batavia's guardian-angel, Eliphas, observes:

‘ From proud Hispania's proud and cruel power
    I've brought her here ;’

And the Prince of Orange is saluted as

‘ The princely youth
    In whom Liberto's name
    Must live or be extinguished.’

persecution and his ill-will towards the Spanish monarchy; and it should be remembered that during the period of his literary activity Spain gradually became once more to Englishmen the most unpopular of foreign powers,[1] and that in 1740, when the masque was printed, she was once more at war with England. Lillo's biblical knowledge, as well as his evidently strong religious sentiment, are partially accounted for by the express statement that he was a dissenter;[2] and his political opinions were no doubt in general agreement with those which at that time prevailed among English Protestant nonconformists.[3]

Lillo is stated to have been brought up as a jeweller, and during a considerable part of his life appears to have carried on this trade in the City of London, where the diamond business is to this day largely in the hands of Dutch merchants. With the City his writings — and not *The London Merchant* only — show him to have been familiar.[4] Whether or not his success as a playwright, which was established with great rapidity on the production of *The London Merchant* in 1731, interfered with the steady progress of his business life, remains uncertain. In his later years, he appears to have resided at Rotherhithe. He died on September 3, 1739, and was buried in the vault of Shoreditch Church. If any reliance is to be

1 See the bitter reference to religious persecution in *The London Merchant*, ll. 65-73, p. 89, and the tirade against Spain in *Fatal Curiosity*, Act I, Sc. I (p. 149).

2 Several apt biblical illustrations will be noted in *The London Merchant*. Lillo's deep religious sentiment is well brought out in his play *The Christian Hero;* see Scanderbeg's prayer, vol. I, p. 249, ed. 1775, and cf. the close of his speech in the opening scene, *idem*, p. 288.

3 See the passage against the theory of Right Divine in *The Christian Hero*, Act V, *ad fin.*, *idem*, p. 301.

4 It is curious that in a purely conceived and finely written passage of *The Christian Hero*, *idem*, p. 269, Lillo should have introduced a graphic reminiscence of the darkest aspect of the London streets. See also the reference in *The London Merchant*, ll. 35-47, p. 88, to the blackmail levied by corrupt London (non-City) magistrates.

placed on a couplet in Hammond's *Prologue* to Lillo's *Elmerick*, posthumously printed in 1740 —

> ' Deprest by want, afflicted by disease,
> Dying he wrote, and dying wish'd to please '—

he must have fallen into or have been overtaken by pecuniary difficulties at some time previous to his death. But the passage may be nothing but a fictitious appeal *ad misericordiam* — especially if the statement of the *Biographia Dramatica* be authentic, that he ' died possessed of an estate of £40 per annum, besides other effects of a considerable value.' The same authority describes him as ' in person lusty, but not tall ; and of a pleasing aspect, though unhappily deprived of the sight of one eye.' Davies, who must have known him personally, speaks of his gentle manners ; and in the *Lives of the Poets*, purporting to be by Theophilus Cibber, he is stated to have been ' a man of strict morals, great good-nature and sound sense, with an uncommon share of modesty.' But his personal worth is best attested by the tribute to him inserted by Fielding in *The Champion* (February 26, 1739/40). Briefly noticing the production of Lillo's tragedy of *Elmerick*, Fielding says that ' such a Regard to Nature shines through the whole, that it is evident the Author writ less from his Head than from an Heart capable of exquisitely Feeling and Painting human Distresses, but of causing none.' To a rather hyperbolical commendation of Lillo's *Fatal Curiosity*, cited below, he then adds that the author ' had the gentlest and honestest Manners, and, at the same Time, the most friendly and obliging. He had a perfect Knowledge of Human Nature, though his Contempt of all base Means of Application, which are the necessary Steps to great Acquaintance, restrained his Conversation within very narrow Bounds. He had the Spirit of an old *Roman*, joined to the Inno-

cence of a primitive Christian ; he was content with his
little State of Life, in which his excellent Temper of Mind
gave him an Happiness beyond the Power of Riches ; and
it was necessary for his Friends to have a sharp Insight
into his Want of their Services, as well as good Inclinations or Abilities to serve him. In short, he was one of
the best of Men, and those who knew him best will most
regret his Loss.' A finer tribute has rarely been paid by
one high-minded writer to another ; and it came in this
instance with particular force and grace from one who was
to hold the mirror up to human nature at large, as well
as to magistrates in particular.[1]

The following is a list of Lillo's plays in the order of
their production, with brief notes as to those not included
in the present volume. It is due to Lillo that his compe-
tence — to say the least — as a writer of the species of
tragedy accepted by his age should not be altogether
overlooked.

Sylvia, or The Country Burial, first acted at Lincoln's
Inn Fields in 1731, was printed in the same year. This
'opera' is of homespun, and in truth of quite coarse, material, virtue and vice being rather tumbled up together ;
while the unbearably gross scene of the 'country burial'
and the resuscitation of the drunken wife has no connexion
with the plot. There is nothing characteristic of Lillo in
this piece except a certain tendency to sententiousness.

*The London Merchant, or The History of George Barn-
well,* was first acted at Drury Lane June 22, 1731, and
printed in the same year.

The Christian Hero, a regular tragedy in blank verse,
was first acted at Drury Lane in 1734, and printed in the

---

1 As to Fielding's subsequent tribute, in *Joseph Andrews,* to *The London Merchant,* see below, p. xxvii.

same year, with a *Life of Scanderbeg* (the hero of the play), which may, or may not, be Lillo's. This tragedy seems to have given offence to the friends of Whincop, the author of the tragedy of *Scanderbeg* (published after his death in 1747), as an ungenerous plagiarism of his theme ; and the ill-will shows itself in the *List of Dramatic Authors* printed with Whincop's piece, where Lillo is described as 'by profession a Jeweller, but having a strong Inclination for Poetry, which oftentimes is mistaken for Genius.' Lillo's own play, though untouched by poetic fire, and at the height of its action hardly equal to an exposition of the conflict in the hero between love and duty, is something more than wholesome and pure. It has a solid ring, and only becomes stagey when it reaches the episode of the Sultan's daughter, Hellena.

Fatal Curiosity, 'a true Tragedy,' was first acted at the Little Haymarket in 1736, and printed in 1737.

Marina, a Play, in three acts, partly in blank verse, and partly in prose, was first performed at Covent Garden in 1738, and printed in the same year. It may be summarily described as 'taken out' of *Pericles, Prince of Tyre*; but the obscenity is unfortunately kept in.

Arden of Feversham, 'an historical Tragedy,' in blank verse, though said to have been written in 1736, was not published till long after the author's death, in 1762. This by no means commendable adaptation of a powerful original is interesting because of the special association, through *The London Merchant*, of Lillo's name with the development of 'domestic tragedy' in our dramatic literature. But the 'additions' (Alicia's attempt at murder, in Lady Macbeth's manner, in Act II, her remorse and Arden's 'kindness' in Act IV, and his death-scene) may be set down as little else but interpolations. However, as the adaptation was 'finished' by John Hoadley, Lillo cannot be held altogether responsible for it, or chargeable with the authorship of its bald tag.

Elmerick, or Justice Triumphant, published in 1740, is likewise a posthumous tragedy, but of the regular type, and wholly in blank verse. In this finely conceived and well-executed drama, justly praised by Fielding, some traces are recognisable of a masculine conception of virtue, 'public' and private, which ranges above that accepted by his age. Ismena's Lucretia-like narration shows refinement of feeling; and though the diction nowhere rises to poetry, it is devoid neither of passion nor of force.

Of the entertainment *Britannia and Batavia*, printed in 1740, mention has already been made. It does not appear to have been performed. The *dramatis personae* are quite different from those of *Britannia, or The Royal Lovers*, an entertainment given at Goodman's Fields from February, 1734, with a Pastoral Epithalamium, 'The Happy Nuptials,' by Carey introduced in its last scene (Genest, III, 433). A comedy by Lillo called *The Regulators* is stated (in a note to Davies's *Life* in the edition of 1810) to have been 'said to be existing in manuscript, in 1773'; but it has never seen the light.

Introduction

The London Merchant, or The History of George Barnwell, when first acted at Drury Lane on June 22, 1731, seems to have been announced under the title of *The Merchant, or the True History of George Barnwell*. The sub-title in each case clearly shows the author to have desired it to be understood that his play was directly founded upon fact. Conscious of the innovation which this at the time implied, and as a dramatist who had not yet made his way with the public, Lillo seems to have preferred to produce his play on the stage out of the regular theatrical season. Yet, though the critics *ex officio* may have been conspicuous by their absence from the pit at the first performance, and may afterwards have declined to allow their judgment to go simply by default,[1] the arch-critic of the Augustan age is said to have been present on the memorable twenty-second of June, which heralded a literary revolution quite beyond his ken. Pope's criticism is on record[2] that the author of *The London Merchant* had in this play 'never deviated from propriety, except in a few passages in which he aimed at a greater elevation of language than was consistent with the characters and the situation.' In anticipation of the performance, the old ballad of *George Barnwell*, which is

[1] See (Hammond's) *Prologue to Elmerick*:

'His *Barnwell* once no critic's test could bear,
But from each eye still draws the natural tear.'

[2] See the life of Lillo in T. Cibber's *Lives of the Poets of Great Britain and Ireland* (1753), vol. v, p. 339.

reproduced as an appendix,[1] was reprinted in a large
number of copies — many thousands are said to have
been sold in a single day; and the story has often been
repeated, how on the first night many of the intending
spectators had bought a copy for the purpose of making
a 'ridiculous comparison' between it and the play,
but that before the latter was finished, they threw away
their ballads and took out their handkerchiefs.

The part of George Barnwell was on this occasion
played by 'Mr. Cibber, junior' — Theophilus Cibber
(the son of 'King Colley'), whose life, as the *Biographia Dramatica* says with almost literal truth,
'was begun, pursued and ended in a storm.' He was
at the time manager of the summer company at Drury
Lane, of which theatre he was patentee from September, 1731, to June, 1732, in his father's place.
The part of Millwood was taken by Mrs. Butler, who
is found acting with the younger Cibber as late as
1742–3. Genest[2] says that 'little is recorded of her,
but she seems to have been a respectable actress.'
Maria was performed by Mrs. Cibber (Theophilus's
first wife, who died in 1734); she also spoke the
deplorable Epilogue. The part of Lucy was taken by
Mrs. Charke[3] (Colley Cibber's youngest daughter
Charlotte). The play was thoroughly successful, and
was acted for twenty nights to crowded houses. On
July 2, 1731, Queen Caroline, whose moral *flair* was

[1] See p. 122.   [2] *Some Account of the English Stage*, vol. IV, p. 50.

[3] Not Clarke, as given in the *dramatis personae* of some octavos
and the edition of 1810. Mrs. Charke (who acted Mrs. Wilmot
in *Fatal Curiosity* in 1755) was doubtless the same person. Her
name had of old had a Puritan sound in London.

quite equal to her literary insight, sent to Drury Lane
for the manuscript of *The London Merchant* in order to
peruse it; and it was duly carried by Mr. Wicks (who had
not been in the cast) to Hampton Court. The manager
Cibber behaved liberally to Lillo, procuring for him a
fourth benefit-night in the winter season, so that he
netted a sum of several thousand pounds by the success
of his piece, which continued a stock play while Cibber
remained connected with Drury Lane. It came to be
frequently acted in the Christmas and Easter holidays,
being esteemed a better entertainment for the city prentices than the coarse shows with which they were at
such seasons habitually regaled on the stage; and this
tradition, notwithstanding Charles Lamb's protest,[1]
lingered on to a comparatively recent day.[2]

[1] In a footnote to his essay *On the Tragedies of Shakespeare*,
which, as his editor A. Ainger truly observes, 'contains some
of the noblest criticism ever written,' and from which an example
of such criticism, though uncomplimentary to Lillo, will be quoted
in my text. 'If,' says Lamb, 'this note could hope to meet the
eye of any of the Managers, I would entreat and beg of them, in
the name of both the galleries, that this insult upon the morality
of the common people of London should cease to be eternally
repeated in the holiday weeks. Why are the 'Prentices of this
famous and well-governed city, instead of an amusement, to be
treated over and over again with a nauseous sermon of George Barnwell? Why *at the end of their vistas* are we to place the *gallows?*
Were I an uncle I should not much like a nephew of mine to
have such an example placed before his eyes. It is really making
uncle-murder too trivial to exhibit it as done upon such slight motives; — it is attributing too much to such characters as Millwood;
it is putting things into the heads of good young men, which they
would never otherwise have dreamed of. Uncles that think anything of their lives, should fairly petition the Chamberlain against it.'

[2] I can remember *The London Merchant* being thus annually

On December 26, 1751, and afterwards, the part of George Barnwell was played at Drury Lane by David Ross (that of Millwood being taken by Mrs. Pritchard, who may not have felt it necessary to be too 'genteel' on the occasion); and many years afterwards this gifted actor (whose own youthful indiscretion had led his father to cut him off with an annual shilling 'to put him in mind of the misfortune he had to be born') told a curious story in connexion with this impersonation. About the time of the revival of the play, Dr. Barrowby [1] was sent for to the apprentice of a 'capital merchant'; when this youth confessed to the physician that in consequence of an illicit amour he had embezzled two hundred pounds of his master's money, but that since witnessing a few nights previously the performance of *George Barnwell* he had not had a moment's peace and desired to die so as to avoid the shame of discovery. Dr. Barrowby intervened; the apprentice's father paid the money, and for nine or ten years anonymously sent to Ross an annual present of ten guineas as a tribute of gratitude.

played at the Theatre Royal, Manchester. Sir Henry Irving, when a member of the stock company at that theatre, at the beginning of a career which was not only full of honours for himself but most beneficent to the national stage, frequently played George Barnwell. How I wish that, like our common friend Mr. E. J. Broadfield, to whom Sir Henry mentioned this fact, I could have heard the great actor repeat the speech, which late in life he could still recall, of the unhappy youth on his way to execution.

[1] If this was the celebrated (or notorious) Dr. Barrowby, there must be some error of date, as this personage — with whose reported character the story does not appear to be altogether in keeping — died, according to Dr. Norman Moore in the *Dictionary of National Biography*, on December 30, 1751.

In 1796, *The London Merchant*, after remaining unperformed for seven years, was revived, with Charles Kemble in the hero's part, and no less a personage than Mrs. Siddons (who had thought that the revival might be to her brother's advantage) in that of Millwood.

The printed editions of this play are extremely numerous; not less than 22 are to be found in the British Museum, and to these not less than four have to be added following the first and second, and preceding the seventh (in 1740). In the first and second editions, both of which appeared in the year of the first production of the play on the stage, the last act consists of eleven scenes, of which the tenth ends with Barnwell's departure to execution, and the eleventh is the short scene, which concludes the play in all the editions, between Blunt, Lucy, and Trueman. The intervening scene, which is laid at the place of execution, with the gallows at the further end of the stage, appears to have been performed on the stage for several years, but then to have been laid aside, till it was reintroduced on the revival of the play at Bath in 1817. Genest [1] adds that the fifth ' genuine edition ' of the play was announced for publication on February 8, 1735 (N. S.) ' with a new Frontispiece, from an additional scene, never before printed.' [2] The additional scene appears in the edition of

---

[1] *Some Account of the English Stage*, vol. III, pp. 295–6.

[2] This edition is not in the British Museum ; and the scene is printed in the present volume from the edition of 1740. The frontispiece may be the original of the sorry woodcut prefixed to the reprint of *George Barnwell* in vol. IX of Cumberland's *British Theatre* (1826). All endeavours to discover this edition or an engraving of a scene in the play have proved unsuccessful.

the play of 1740, and in both Gray's and Davies's collective editions of Lillo's Works, but in none of the single editions of the play, so far as they have been verified, after that of 1768.

The story of *The London Merchant*, to which the play assigns the date of Queen Elizabeth's reign, not long before the sailing of the Great Armada, is (as already observed) presented by the author as a reproduction of actual events. It had manifestly been suggested to Lillo by the old ballad already mentioned, which is to be found in Bishop Percy's *Reliques of Ancient English Poetry*[1] and in *English and Scottish Ballads*, selected and edited by F. J. Child,[2] from which latter it is here reprinted as an appendix. Bishop Percy observes : 'As for the ballad, it was printed at least as early as the middle of the 17th century. It is here given from three old printed copies, which exhibit a strange intermixture of Roman and black-letter. It is also collated with another copy in the Ashmole Collection at Oxford, entitled : " *An Excellent Ballad of George Barnwell, an apprentice of London, who thrice robb'd his master, and murdered his uncle in Ludlow*." The tune is *The Merchant*.' Professor Child adds : 'There is another copy in Ritson's *Ancient Songs*, ii, 156. Throughout the Second Part, the first line of each stanza has, in the old editions, two superfluous syllables, which Percy ejected ; and Ritson has adopted the emendation.'

It will be seen that, while there is a general agreement between ballad and play, the former contains

---

[1] Vol. iii, pp. 297 *seqq*. Ed. Wheatley, 3 vols. 1876–7.
[2] Vol. viii, pp. 213 *seqq*. Boston, 1859.

nothing as to the virtuous attachment of the master's daughter for Barnwell, or as to the friendship of his fellow apprentice; while with regard to Barnwell himself, the story in the ballad takes a different close, sending him out to meet his fate 'in Polonia,' instead of bringing him to justice in company with his paramour at home. It is difficult, if not impossible, to resist the conclusion that the dramatist must have had access to some source or sources of information concerning the story of George Barnwell besides the old ballad itself.

It was probably the *éclat* given to the reputation of Lillo's play by the Kemble revival of it in 1796 which led to the publication of a three-volume novel by T. S. Surr, entitled *Barnwell,* which is dedicated to Mrs. Siddons, and of which, in its fourth edition (London, 1807), a copy is to be found in the British Museum.[1] That the author has caught the spirit of the dramatist's purpose is shown by the motto from Cowper which he prefixes to his story:

> ' Studious of song,
> And yet ambitious not to sing in vain,
> I would not trifle merely ';

but in the course of the novel he is said to have deviated from the facts on which it is based more than Lillo himself had done in his play.

Are these facts to be found in a narrative, treating poor Barnwell's affair with much didactic exuberance, which

---

[1] Of Thomas Skinner Surr, who died in 1847, a short but curious account is given in the *Dictionary of National Biography*, vol. LV. He was a prosperous City man and a successful novelist, who knew the value of direct portraiture in fiction.

was published not long afterwards and of which the Preface ? is dated ' St. Gads, December 21, 1809 ' ? [1] In this version of the story, which claims to possess unimpeachable authority, there is a profusion of personal and local names. The hero is a native of ' the Vale of Evesham, where the family of the Barnwells flourished.' The good merchant to whom the youth was apprenticed was ' Mr. Strickland, a very considerable woollen-draper in Cheapside.' Barnwell has two fellow apprentices named Thorowgood and Trueman, whereas in the play the former of these names, which might seem to have come straight from Bunyan,[2] is given to the Merchant. As to the evil heroine of the tragedy, the *Memoirs* state that Sarah was the daughter of a respectable merchant at Bristol, where, instead of dutifully marrying a Mr. Vaughan, she ran away with a less respectable member of society named Millwood, who with her assistance set up a barber's shop ' near the Gun ' in Shoreditch, but not long afterwards ' lost his life in a midnight broil ' ; whereupon she converted their house into a brothel. The ' general residence '

---

[1] *Memoirs of George Barnwell, the unhappy subject of Lillo's celebrated Tragedy, derived from the most authentic source, and intended for the perusal and instruction of the Rising Generation.* By a Descendant of the Barnwell Family. Printed at Harlow [in Essex] by B. Flower for W. Jones . . . of No. 5, Newgate Street, London, 1810. An abridgment of this was published (London, 1820) under the title of *The Life and History of George Barnwell*, etc.

[2] That Thoroughgood was a real name is oddly enough shown by an advertisement, in my copy of the *Memoirs*, of a story or tract against juvenile infidelity and vice, entitled *Philario and Clarinda*, and purporting to be by ' the late Rev. John Thorowgood.'

of Barnwell's uncle was at Camberwell in Surrey; and the murder of him took place in Camberwell Grove. After the deed had been done, the old gentleman's body was carried to an old public-house hard by, 'well known by the sign of the Tiger and the Tabby.' Millwood received the assassin graciously : 'I have a little leisure now to listen to you ; how did the old codger meet his fate ?' A brief, but telling, account is given of Barnwell's subsequent flight to Nottingham and Lincoln, where he is apprehended by the messengers of justice to whom Mr. Strickland had imparted Millwood's information. In Newgate George Barnwell opens his mind to the Ordinary, who 'was extremely attentive to him, and in writing down the particulars of his past life, for the benefit of young men who should themselves feel tempted to leave the paths of integrity and virtue.' This chaplain has not handed down his notes ; but it is tantalising that it should apparently be impossible to control the further statement of this narrative, that Barnwell was tried at the Kingston assizes on October 18, 1706, before Chief Baron Bury and Mr. Justice Powel, Mr. Wainwright being counsel for the Crown, and Mr. Price with him. The trial attracted a very numerous audience ; 'fathers, and others who had the care of the rising generation, came with their offspring and protégés, hoping much from the development of the progress of vice which would take place, and the wretched appearance of the victim.' Sarah Millwood, Robert Thorowgood, Thomas Trueman, and other witnesses were examined. The speeches of counsel are condensed, but the convict's edifying speech at the close is given in full.[1] He was sentenced to be hung in chains on Kennington Common, and his speech at the gallows is likewise included in the *Memoirs*, which furnish no clue as to Millwood's ultimate fate.

The significance of the production of Lillo's *London Merchant* for the history of the modern, and in the first instance for that of the English, drama lies in his choice of subject and, though perhaps not in the same measure, in his choice of form. The last spark of originality seemed to have died out of English tragedy, together with the last trace of an occasional reaction towards the freedom of the Elizabethans; and the dead level of mere imitation of French classical models had remained undisturbed by the gentle eminences reached in the more successful of the dramatic works of Ambrose Philips, Charles Johnson, Fenton and Hughes, in the *Sophonisba* of Thomson, and in Young's *Busiris* and *The Revenge*. In his present endeavour, Lillo renounced all aspirations for a theme worthy of

    ' *Tragoedia cothurnata*, fitting kings ' ;

[1] There is nothing in Lillo's play which directly recalls this speech. It is singular that of a trial of which time, place, and the names of the presiding judges are given (William Bury died as Chief Baron of the Exchequer in 1716, Sir John Powell as a Judge in the Exchequer in 1713), no record should appear to be accessible. But a communication to *Notes and Queries* (2 Ser., vol. v, 1858), stating that the writer had never met with any authenticated notice of the trial and condemnation of George Barnwell, elicited no response ; and my own enquiries have proved equally unsuccessful. It appears that no record exists of ordinary criminal trials held at so early a date, except occasionally in newspapers.

and, reaching forth his hand no further than the seeth-ing human life immediately around him, thereby set an example of which, for better for worse, the modern drama has never since lost sight. At the same time, as an almost inevitable consequence of his choice of sub-ject, he reclaimed for himself the use of prose, as the dramatic form alone appropriate for his purpose, and so removed another of the shackles which English trag-edy, 'hugging the chain she clanked,' had chosen to impose upon herself.

It was thus that Lillo, by what to himself and his contemporaries seemed an innovation, gave a new and enduring vitality to the dramatic species known in literary history as 'domestic tragedy.' Of course, neither the extension of the range of the tragic drama into the sphere of every-day popular life, nor the use of prose as the vehicle of a tragic action, was a new thing in the history of the English theatre. It should, moreover, be noted that Lillo did not venture so far as to move the time at which his tragedy played forward to his own day. In the opening scene he takes care to make it clear that the time of the action is the reign of Elizabeth ; and it is even dated with a certain precision as not long before the sailing of the great Spanish Ar-mada, when a loan for meeting the expenses of its outfit is supposed to have been refused to Philip by the Genoese.[1]

[1] There is probably no kind of historical foundation for this re-fusal. At the time in question the influence of Spain was dominant at Genoa, though King Philip could not meet the pecuniary obli-gations which he had incurred there.

Elizabethan tragedy had never disdained the treatment of themes derived from the actual, more or less contemporary, life of ordinary English society. Such a play was the very notable *Arden of Feversham* (afterwards adapted by Lillo himself) which was printed in 1592, but had probably been acted some seven years earlier. It is a dramatic version of the story of the murder of a Kentish gentleman, related by Holinshed, which had possibly already served as the theme of a previous play, *Murderous Michael* (1578). Both Tieck and Ulrici thought Shakspere's hand discernible in *Arden of Feversham*; and the play certainly contains passages which recall his touch. Another extant early play of the same description is *A Warning for Fair Women* (1599). In the first decade of the seventeenth century several plays of the same or a similar type were published: among them *The London Prodigal*, printed in 1605, which contains the pathetic character of the faithful Luce. Lessing appears to have considered this play Shaksperean, and to have intended to adapt it for the German stage. Another play of the class of *Arden of Feversham* is *A Yorkshire Tragedy* (printed in 1608), a powerful dramatisation of a horrible story of real life, which Schlegel believed to be by Shakspere's hand, but which Hazlitt thought rather in Thomas Heywood's manner. Thomas Heywood's undoubted masterpiece in the species of the domestic drama, *A Woman Killed with Kindness* (acted not later than 1603), is true in colouring, and rises to a high pitch of tragic power in the thrilling scene of the husband's unexpected return to his polluted home. Among

later Elizabethan (or Jacobean) plays of a similar kind
may be included George Wilkins's *Miseries of Enforced
Marriage* (printed 1607), and perhaps also Dekker
and Ford's *Witch of Edmonton* (printed 1658, but
probably produced in 1621).

The tone and temper of the earlier Restoration drama
could hardly favour the treatment of themes of domestic
intimacy and trouble; but towards the close of the century a reaction in this direction set in with Thomas
Southerne's *The Fatal Marriage, or The Innocent Adul-
tery* (1694), afterwards revived under the name of
Isabella, but known to so modern a young lady as
Miss Lydia Languish under its more captivating title.
This is a tragic version of an extremely long-lived
literary theme, most widely familiar to modern readers
through Tennyson's *Enoch Arden*, and bordering on
the story of Lillo's own *Fatal Curiosity*. The interest in pathetic subjects of this description was kept
alive by some of the tragedies of Rowe — such as *The
Fair Penitent*, with the original Lothario — and more
especially of Otway — *The Orphan* in particular. But
the beginnings of Sentimental Comedy did not make
their appearance on the English stage till some years
later. Colley Cibber, in his *Careless Husband*, produced in 1704, professed to have deliberately sought
' to reform by example the coarseness of contemporary
comedy ' ; and to this end made the pathetic treatment
of a moral purpose the basis of the action of this play.
He cannot, however, be said to have carried much
further the experiment which his theatrical instinct
had suggested to him. The Dedication of his comedy

The Lady's Last Stake, or The Wife's Resentment
(1708) declares that 'a Play without a just Moral is
a poor and trivial undertaking'; but the piece cannot
be classed as a sentimental comedy, though it ends with
the return of husband and wife to a mutual affection.
Of his later plays, *The Provoked Husband* (1728),
an adaptation of Vanbrugh's *Journey to London*, provided this unsentimental comedy with a sentimental
ending, largely written in iambics (so that coals of fire
were heaped on the head of Vanbrugh, who in his
Relapse had given an immoral turn to the plot of Cibber's first comedy, *Love's Last Shift*). Meanwhile
the hint given by Cibber's *Careless Husband* was taken
and bettered by Steele. After, in his *Lying Lover*
(1703), he had made a serious and pathetic addition
of his own, in blank verse, to the action of Corneille's
Menteur, he in 1705 produced *The Tender Husband*,
a comedy in which virtuous affection between husband
and wife is introduced as a dramatic motive. His *Conscious Lovers* (1722), in which the main interest of the
comedy is sentimental, may be reckoned as a full-blown
example of the new species.

About the same time, it was being assiduously cultivated in France, where already Corneille had shown,
by example as well as by precept, that the sorrowings
and sufferings of people of our own class, or near to
it, touch us more nearly than the griefs of kings and
queens. The French growth was more abundant, but
in this period hardly went beyond English precedent,
and was in part influenced by it. Destouches, whose
first acted comedy dates from 1710, resided in Eng-

land from 1717–23 (three years before Voltaire's famous visit) and married an English wife. His *Philosophe marié* (1727) — afterwards reproduced on the English stage in 1732 in a version by John Kelley — is a comedy with a serious basis and a morally satisfactory ending; and in his later productions he pursued the same vein — from *Le Glorieux* (1732), in which there is a suggestion of *Timon*, to *Le Dissipateur* (1753), which is (to speak theatrically rather than ethically) a serious drama in a comic form. More notable, from a literary point of view, are the delightful dramatic productions of Marivaux; but even his masterpiece, the imperishable *Jeu de l' Amour et du Hasard* (1730), whose grace and elegance are made perfect by a gentle undercurrent of pathos, is not so much a sentimental comedy as a comedy with sentiment in it. The transition to sentimental comedy proper, and the slight supplementary step to the *comédie larmoyante* — in which very rare comic islets are left floating in a sea of tears — were achieved by Nivelle de la Chaussée. He still adhered to the use of verse (for which his clever *Epître à Clio* is a very agreeable apology), but in his comedy *La Fausse Antipathie* (1734) the sentiment already predominates over the gaiety; and, alike in the Prologue prefixed to it, and in the *Critique* with which according to custom he followed it up, he presents himself as the conscious representative of a school of dramatists in search of what is true, natural, and 'dramatic to a fault.' His *Ecole des Amis* (1737), his *Melanide* (1741), and his *Ecole des Mères* (1744), form a series of tributes to virtue and the *status quo ante bellum*, and are all more or less amenable to Frederick the Great's objection against turning the stage into a *bureau de fadeur*. But Frederick's own philosopher and friend, Voltaire himself, had occasionally shown an inclination to essay the new style; witness passages of his comedy *L'Enfant Prodigue* (1736) and the whole argument of his *Nanine, ou Le Préjugé Vaincu* (1746), which is taken direct from Richardson's *Pamela*, of which subject, afterwards a favourite stage theme of the Revolution age, Nivelle de la Chaussée's dramatic version, *Paméla*, had appeared six years earlier (1743).

Meanwhile, it should be noted that while in some of the plays of the above-named French writers sentimental comedy and its excess, *comédie larmoyante*, already rubbed shoulders with domestic tragedy,[1] there is nothing in these or in any contemporary productions to deprive Lillo's most important work of its title to originality; indeed the large majority of these plays were actually later in date than *The London Merchant*. It is quite true that the moral growth and social expansion in the life of the English middle-class, which was closely connected with its political advance, in the early Georgian period — the increased regard paid in this age to the demands of religion and morality, the combination

---

[1] Voltaire, in his preface to the 'bagatelle,' as he calls it, of *Nanine* distinguishes sentimental from 'tearful' comedy. He says: 'Comedy, I repeat, may have its moods of passion, anger, and melting pity, provided that it afterwards makes well-bred people laugh. If it were to lack the comic element and to be only tearful (*larmoyante*), it is then that it would be a very faulty and very disagreeable species.'

of a fuller tolerance in matters of belief with a greater
rigour in the conduct of life in some of its aspects, and
notably as to the relations between the sexes, together
with the influence exercised in most of these directions
by the improved social position of Protestant nonconformists, made themselves felt in many branches of the
national literature and art. Most notably was such the
case in English prose fiction, as entirely recast in spirit
as well as in form by Richardson, and in pictorial art
as nationalised, and at the same time 'moralised,' by
Hogarth. But it should be remembered that these
changes did not precede, but followed, Lillo's innovation on the stage; for *Pamela* was not published till
1740, and Hogarth's earliest important work (*The
Harlot's Progress*) was not issued to subscribers till
1732.[1]

The brilliant success of Lillo's play on the English
stage and the remarkable attention bestowed upon his
effort in France, Holland, and more especially in Germany (of which there will be something further to
say), was no doubt primarily due to his choice of
subject, and to the direct appeal thus made to the
business and bosoms of the spectators and readers of his

---

[1] In his *Joseph Andrews* (1742) Fielding, in the humorous
dialogue between the poet and the player (bk. III, ch. 10) puts
into the mouth of the latter the following ironical depreciation of
the tragic poets of his own generation; ' . . . . but yet, to do justice
to the actors, what could Booth or Betterton have made of such
horrible stuff as Fenton's Marianne, Frowde's Philotas, or Mallet's
Eurydice, or those low, dirty, " last dying speeches," which a fellow in the City or Wapping, your Dillo or Lillo (what was his
name), called tragedies? '

tragedy. *The London Merchant* undeniably falls short
of the definition of tragedy implied in the admirably
expressed statement by a distinguished living critic of
both the ancient and the modern drama, that 'every
tragic action consists of a great crisis in some great life,
not merely narrated but presented in act, through language, in such a way as to move the hearts of those
who see and hear.' [1] The greatness of the life, as
well as the greatness of the crisis in it — and in each
case a greatness which, to quote the same writer, is
'at once outward and inward'— is what raises such a
tragedy as *Othello* out of the region of the domestic
drama in which some critics have thought themselves
warranted in including it. Charles Lamb, though from
a slightly different point of view, has said much the
same thing in his own inimitable way; and, though
in my opinion the passage reflects somewhat severely
on the shortcomings of Lillo's treatment, it is too
admirable in substance not to be once more quoted at
length:

'It is common for people to talk of Shakspere's plays being so *natural*, that everybody can understand him. They
are natural indeed, they are grounded deep in nature, so
deep that the depth of them lies out of the reach of most
of us. You shall hear the same persons say that *George
Barnwell* is very natural, and *Othello* is very natural, that
they are both very deep ; and to them they are the same
kind of thing. At the one they sit and shed tears, because a good sort of young man is tempted by a naughty

---

[1] See Professor Lewis Campbell's *Tragic Drama in Æschylus,
Sophocles and Shakespeare* (1904), p. 29.

woman to commit *a trifling peccadillo*, the murder of an uncle or so, that is all, and so comes to an untimely end, which is so *moving* ; and at the other, because a blackamoor in a fit of jealousy kills his innocent white wife : and the odds are that ninety-nine out of a hundred would willingly behold the same catastrophe happen to both the heroes, and have thought the rope more due to Othello than to Barnwell. For of the texture of Othello's mind, the inward construction marvellously laid open with all its strength and weaknesses, its heroic confidences and its human misgivings, its agonies of hate springing from the depths of love, they see no more than the spectators at a cheaper rate, who pay their pennies apiece to look through the man's telescope in Leicester Fields, see into the inward plot and topography of the moon. Some dim thing or other they see, they see an actor personating a passion, of grief, of anger, for instance, and they recognize it as a copy of the usual external effects of such passions ; or at least as being true to that symbol of the emotion which passes current at the theatre for it, for it is often no more than that : but of the grounds of the passion, its correspondence to a great or heroic nature, which is the only worthy object of tragedy — that common auditors know anything of this . . . I can neither believe, nor understand how it can be possible.' [1]

Whether, within the limits of his subject, Lillo can be said to display dramatic power of a high kind, is a question as to which I should not be prepared to allow judgment to go by default. There can be no doubt that although the characters of this play are taken from actual life, they are for the most part devoid of that inherent vividness which impresses us when human

---

[1] *On the Tragedies of Shakspere.*

nature reveals its hidden depths under the searchlight of an awful calamity, of a great moral trial. Not only the eminently respectable London merchant, his blameless daughter, and Barnwell's friend — the very model of a virtuous apprentice — are of the stage, stagey; but there is no touch of poetry to soften the very truthful and very painful picture of Barnwell's own loss of the innocence which leaves the soul free. On the other hand, certain touches in the personality of the heartless harlot Millwood, and the suggestion at least of an impressive though daring apology for her wickedness, gave to this character a vitality of its own and prevented it from being submerged with the play to which it belonged. It must, moreover, be conceded that in the scenes where the dramatic action rises to its height, Lillo avoids redundancy of speech, and sustains the attention of reader or spectator by the force of the situation itself. Beyond this he does not go, at least in this tragedy, where he neither seeks nor finds an opportunity for essaying one of those subtler studies of the wild vagaries into which human nature deviates when corrupted by crime, or of the depths of elemental feeling which terror, remorse, and self-pity are capable of sounding — such as, in dealing with such themes, writers far inferior in power to Dickens, or even to Dostoïeffsky, have succeeded in stamping upon our imaginations. He can hardly have been held, even by an age not averse like our own to lengthy moralisings, to have made up for these shortcomings, in many passages of his piece, by a sententiousness which must have been like a second nature to him, since traces of it appear in all his dramatic productions, from the earliest and least commendable of them onwards. Not that this habit invariably lands him in platitudes even when he indulges it, for clearness of didactic expression is in him by no means always accompanied by shallowness, and his favourite storehouse of gnomic illustrations is the Bible.

Very possibly, the popularity of Lillo's play was in the first instance enhanced by his use of prose instead of verse throughout the dialogue. Clearly a theme taken from every-day life is in an English drama — and probably in a German, while French dramatic verse stands on a somewhat different footing — most satisfactorily treated without a metrical transformation of the language in which it is clothed ;[1] nor can Johnson's plea to the contrary be regarded as other than paradoxical. That illustrious critic 'could hardly consider a prose tragedy as dramatic; it was difficult for the performers to speak it ; let it be either in the middling or in low life, it might, though in metre and spirited, be properly familiar and colloquial ; many in the middling rank were not without erudition ; they had the feelings and sensations of nature, and every emotion in consequence thereof, as well as the great ; even the

---

[1] Diderot, in his essay *De la Poésie Dramatique* cited below, puts the matter admirably (section x) : 'I have sometimes asked myself whether domestic tragedy might be written in verse, and, without particularly knowing why, have answered, no. . . . Is it, perhaps, that this species requires a particular style of which I have no notion ? Or that the truth of the subject treated and the violence of the interest excited reject a symmetrised form of speech ? Or is it that the status of the *dramatis personae* is too near to our own, to admit of a harmony according to rule ?'

lowest, when impassioned, raised their language ; and the writing of prose was generally the plea and excuse of poverty of genius.' [1]   It will scarcely be thought a corroboration of Johnson's paradox that in *The London Merchant* Lillo largely falls into the practice of writing blank verse which he prints as prose. [2]   This practice, for which precedents were to be found near at hand in Cibber, must, whether consciously adopted or not, be unhesitatingly set down as a fault in art, since it confuses the perceptions of the hearer by a wilful mixture of forms — although it is a fault frequently committed by writers of picturesque prose, and even by so great a master as Dickens.

We may safely conclude that the audiences which crowded to the early performances of *The London Merchant* troubled themselves little about either the artistic defects or the artistic merits of the play. What they welcomed in Lillo's tragedy was, in the first instance, the courage with which, resuming the native freedom of the English drama, he had chosen his theme from a sphere of experience immediately familiar to them ; and, secondly, the plainness of the moral which he enforced, and the direct way in which he enforced it. As will be seen from the prefatory Dedication prefixed by Lillo to his published play, Lillo was quite aware of what he had accomplished on both these heads; but

[1] In Johnson's remarks to G. E. Howard, on receiving from him his play of *The Female Gamester*, in Baker's *Biographia Dramatica, s. v. The Gamester.*

[2] See especially the last Scene of Act III, and the prison-scene in the last Act.

he showed himself to have been aiming at a wrong mark when he declared that he had 'attempted to enlarge the province of the graver kind of poetry. . . . Plays, founded on moral tales in private life, may be of admirable use by carrying conviction to the mind with such irresistible force as to engage all the faculties and powers of the soul in the cause of virtue, by stifling vice in its first principles.' True criticism, while recognising the great service boldly rendered by Lillo to dramatic art by legitimately vindicating to it the right of ranging over as wide as possible an area of subjects, cannot of course set its approval upon his avowed intention to force that art into the service of morality, and to turn the actor into a week-day preacher. Hettner, in the masterly section of his standard work on the history of eighteenth century literature devoted by him to the movement originated by Lillo,[1] quotes a passage from a letter written by Goethe to Meyer in 1793, which puts this matter at once so succinctly and so completely that it may well be re-quoted here : 'The old song of the Philistine, that art must acknowledge the moral law and subordinate itself to it, contains not more than a half-truth. Art has always recognised that law, and must always recognise it, because the laws of art, like the moral law, are derived from reason; but if art were to subordinate itself to morals, it were better for her that a millstone were hanged about her neck and that she were drowned in the depths of the sea, than that she should be doomed to

---

[1] *Litteraturgeschichte des 18 Jahrhunderts*, vol. 1, p. 514 *seqq.* (edition of 1865).

die away gradually into the platitude of a utilitarian purpose.'

But the age on which Lillo (though the actual term was not invented by him or by any other English writer or critic) bestowed the gift of *domestic tragedy* as a new dramatic species was, in the glow of its sentimental and humanitarian enthusiasm, impervious to the fear of any such purely æsthetic danger. On the English stage, where, as has been seen, Lillo had in truth only restored the freedom of an earlier and more spacious era, no great school of dramatists availed itself of the re-emancipation (if it may be so called) achieved by him; but not the less, even though he himself returned to its beaten track, was the ascendancy of blank-verse tragedy on the French model henceforth doomed to gradual extinction. Lillo's *Fatal Curiosity*, as we shall see, besides his brace of adaptations from the Elizabethan drama, followed in the track of his earliest tragedy; and before long Edward Moore, in his monotonous, but tear-compelling prose tragedy of *The Gamester* (1753), provided the English stage with a second stock-piece of essentially the same class as *The London Merchant* — not less simple in its psychology and stilted in its rhetoric, but more clearly cut in form and even more signally exhibiting the force of action in a play. Comedy still maintained its general ascendancy in the productions of our dramatic literature; but the sentimental variety continued to predominate, and was only scotched, not killed, by the touch of nature supplied by Goldsmith. Richard Cumberland, who possessed a genuine power of characterisation, may be said to have carried on the dramatic species reintroduced by Lillo; but he at the same time, so to speak, broke it off as a tragic growth by yielding to a demand which (until these latter days) the theatrical public has persisted in preferring — the demand for a so-called 'happy ending.' Thus on the English stage, too, the species accomplished the evolution through which it passed in the French and in the German theatre.

Both of these were, as a matter of fact, far more strongly affected by Lillo's innovation than was our own, but even they in different degrees. In France, as has been already mentioned, the tendency of several successful dramatists more or less contemporary with him was to give prominence in comedy to an appeal to moral sentiment. It is clear that Lillo's play directly contributed towards the actual transformation of the *comédie larmoyante* into the ulterior species, in which the comic element was practically extinguished, and nothing remained but a direct appeal to morality and the emotions. In 1748 there was published at Paris a French version of *The London Merchant* by Pierre Clément, who, born at Geneva in 1707, had relinquished his duties as a Calvinist minister to become tutor at Paris to the children of Earl Waldegrave, British ambassador at that court. He afterwards accompanied them to England and Italy; and having then devoted himself at Paris to literary pursuits, including the production of plays, was invited by the Church authorities at Geneva to resign his title of minister. In 1767 he died insane at Charenton. Among his plays were two translations from the English, one of which was *Le*

Marchand de Londres.[1] It reached a second edition in
1751; and there can be no doubt that to its direct
influence upon Diderot was largely due the production
of the plays by which he deliberately sought to revolu-
tionise the French theatre, and which occupy an important place in its history as well as in that of dramatic
literature in general. The earlier of these plays, *Le
Fils Naturel,* published in 1757, was at once followed
by the three *Entretiens,* dialogues in which Diderot
expounds his dramatic principles and their application
to his recent production, and in which he twice refers
to Lillo's play as typical of the species which he is
endeavouring to introduce.[2] In 1758 followed *Le Père
de Famille,* accompanied by the *Discours sur la poésie
dramatique,* addressed to Grimm, in the tenth section
of which the theory of domestic tragedy and its application by himself is fully expounded. In 1760, Diderot
composed an adaptation of Moore's *Gamester,* but as
in 1762 a translation of this piece was printed by the
Abbé Bruté de Loirette, Diderot's version remained
unpublished till 1819.[3] His own early association of

[1] The other, *La Double Métamorphose* (1749), was a version of
the celebrated ballad opera by some half a dozen authors, *The Devil
to Pay.*

[2] In *Entretien* I, he eulogises the natural pathos of the prison-
scene between Barnwell and Maria in Act v of *The London Merchant.* (See note *in loc.*) In *Entretien* II, Dorval, after claiming
for the new species the title of 'tragédie domestique et bourgeoise,
adds: 'The English have *The Merchant of London* and *The Gamester,* tragedies in prose. The tragedies of Shakespeare are half
verse, half prose.'

[3] *Le Joueur. Drame imité de l'Anglais.*

The Gamester with *The London Merchant* had led to a general and long-enduring belief in France that Moore's drama was by Lillo. But the amplest extant tribute by Diderot to Lillo occurs in the *Correspondence* of Grimm, who speaks of the great success of *The London Merchant* in England, and its high reputation in France since the publication of the French translation of it. He adds a *critique* by Diderot on the *Epître de Barnevelt*, by Claude-Joseph Dorat, a writer of quite inexhaustible fecundity, supposed to be written from prison by Barnwell (or, more metrically, 'Barnevelt') to his friend 'Truman,' expanding into a 'heroic' epistle the narrative of his parricidal crime. Diderot falls into the trap of confounding the excellent Thoroughgood (softened into 'Sorogoud') with Barnwell's unhappy uncle; but no better critical page was ever written than that distinguishing the lifelike method of Lillo from the pedantries of his adapter.[1]

Beyond a doubt Diderot's dramatic 'innovation' would not have exercised the effect actually produced by it but for the great name of the editor of the *Encyclopédie*, and for the general fermentation of ideas into the midst of which it was cast. Equally beyond a doubt, this effect was literary rather than theatrical, so far as France itself was concerned. *Le Fils Naturel*, though performed at the Duc d'Ayen's private theatre at St. Germain (where, in 1764, was also acted a French version of Lessing's *Miss Sara Sampson*) was not brought on the

---

[1] *Extrait de la Correspondance de Grimm, 1er avril 1764*, in *Miscellanea Dramatiques : La Lettre de Barnevelt; Œuvres de Diderot*, VIII (Belles-Lettres, v), 449 *seqq.* (Paris, 1875).

boards of the *Comédie Française* till 1771, where (with
the help of all the actors except Molé) it proved a
failure.¹ But its literary success was remarkable ; and
it has been well said that no impartial spectator could
have failed to find in it a hitherto undiscovered pathos
and a power which made it possible to forget the stage.
At the same time Lessing justly censured in it a certain
preciosity and an occasional pedantry of philosophical
formulæ. In *Le Père de Famille* the domestic drama
shook itself free from these adventitious elements ; but
though the earlier acts are fine and flowing, — full of
the 'movement' in which Diderot himself thought the
play superior to its predecessor, — and though the whole
drama exhibits a conflict of souls rather than of mere
words, the psychological interest is gradually more or
less dissipated, and the end of the action falls flat. It
was moderately successful on the Paris stage, when
produced there in 1761, after being acted at Marseilles
in the previous year.² On being reproduced at Paris
in 1769, it met with much favour, as also at Naples in
1773. But though Diderot's influence upon both older
contemporary dramatists (such as Sedaine) and younger
(such as Beaumarchais, who essayed this species in
his earlier, now forgotten plays) was considerable, its
real success was remote. In the end the *drame* — a
name which has no character at all — was to become

¹ It was translated into English under the title of *Dorval, or the
Test of Virtue* (1767).
² It was translated into English in 1770 ; and again in 1781
under the title of *A Family Picture*, by a lady. Its revival on the
Paris stage in 1841 was not successful.

the dominating species of the living French stage, and to survive through all the changes rung upon one another by classicism and romanticism.

In the mean time Diderot had contributed to give force and freedom to the developement of the German drama, in the direction to which all his efforts had tended at home. Lessing, who in 1760 published an anonymous translation of Diderot's plays, and prefixed his name to its second edition in 1781, in the preface to the latter correctly states that Diderot had a greater influence on the German theatre than on that of his own nation.[1] To this influence no writer contributed in anything like the same measure as Lessing himself, both by his translation and by the memorable criticisms of the *Fils Naturel* and the *Père de Famille* and of Diderot's dramatic principles in general in the *Hamburger Dramaturgie*.[2] But it was an influence for the reception of which the soil had been long and diligently prepared in Germany.

Here Gottsched and other faithful devotees of French literary influence by adaptation and imitation assiduously cultivated the dramatic species represented by Marivaux and his successors, and the most popular member of the Leipzig School, Gellert, indited an academical dissertation *Pro comoediâ commovente*, the effect of the innovation on the English stage was even greater than in France. In Germany the movement began at the top, and organically connected itself with the per-

[1] *Gesammelte Werke*, 1858 edn. IV, 360 *seqq.*
[2] Nos. LXXXIV–LXXXVIII. See the annotated edition by F. Schröter and R. Thiele, Halle, 1877, pp. 489 *seqq.*

ception of the potent significance of the English theatre at large, which was beginning to dawn upon the leaders of German literature. The foremost of these leaders in critical courage and insight, as well as in formative promptitude and power, Lessing, seized upon Lillo's domestic tragedy as the model of his own earliest creative effort in the sphere of the drama. That Lillo's play was the model of *Miss Sara Sampson* (1755) would be rendered certain by a comparison of the two works, even had not Lessing given utterance to the awful declaration that he would rather be the author of *The London Merchant* than of *The Dying Cato*. Although the personages in Lessing's drama belong to a rather more elevated class of society than those of Lillo's, *Miss Sara Sampson* is unhesitatingly to be set down as an example of 'middle-class' domestic tragedy. Of course this does not mean that Lessing's play (in which certain of the names and certain elements in the situations are alike taken from *Clarissa Harlowe*) is copied from Lillo's, or even that the monstrous Marwood is, except in her wickedness, tenacity, and furious invective, a copy of the more monstrous Millwood.[1] For the rest, although Lillo's tragedy found its way in a translation to the German reading public before 1772, as it did to that of Holland a few years later,[2] Lessing had by this time, urged by the invigorating and purifying force of his genius, passed on to the

---

[1] See the paper, suggested by Professor Caro's *Lessing und Swift* (Jena, 1869), contributed by me to *Macmillan's Magazine*, vol. xxxv (1876–77).

[2] The British Museum contains copies of *Der Kaufmann von*

creation of *Emilia Galotti* (1772), a powerful drama that soars above the region of domestic tragedy and *bürgerliches Trauerspiel* from which it had issued. Thus he had passed not only beyond Lillo, but beyond Diderot, after with the help of the former anticipating the latter. As late as the years 1779–83, however, *The London Merchant* was still to be seen on the German stage, where in these years the great actor Schröder produced it, though without success, in Hamburg and in some of the other leading German theatres. The *Rührstück,* of which it was the prototype, had too many affinities with certain qualities of the ordinary German mind not to have established itself on the national stage for many a long year to come. Such a play as Iffland's very effective *Verbrechen aus Ehrsucht,* and many another heart-rending production by that actor of genius and author of insight — not to mention the labours of Kotzebue and Frau Birch-Pfeiffer which employed the pocket-handkerchiefs of later generations — may fairly be said to owe their literary paternity to *George Barnwell.* But the freedom which Lillo so materially helped to give to the modern serious drama, and without which it could hardly have been preserved from decrepitude or emasculation, entitles him to a grateful remembrance which no

London, oder Begebenheiten G. Barnwell's. Ein bürgerliches Trauerspiel, aus dem Englischen des Herrn Tillo [*sic*] übersetzt durch H. A. B. Neue Auflage. Hamburg, 1772; of the same in a later edition of 1781; and of *De Koopman von London.* Burgerlyk treurspel, naar het Engelsche van den Heer Tillo [*sic*]. Amsterdam. 1779. Neither the Dutch nor the German translation (of which the former seems to be a version) contains the additional scene to be found in some of the English editions.

abuse of the acquisition ought to affect, and no lapse of time should render obsolete.[1]

Fatal Curiosity, the second of the two plays by Lillo reprinted in the present volume, was first acted at the Little Haymarket, on May 27, 1736, under the title of *Guilt Its Own Punishment, or Fatal Curiosity*. It is stated to have been, on its original production, played seven times.[2] It was announced for its first performance as ' by Pasquin's Company of Comedians. Never acted before. Being a true story in Common Life, and the Incidents extremely affecting. Written by the author of George Barnwell.'[3] The Little Haymarket had then been recently opened by Fielding (who, as

[1] The satire of *George de Barnwell*, Thackeray's travesty in his *Novels by Eminent Hands*, applies, not to Lillo's play, but to certain of the earlier writings of Lord Lytton ; the hero is a representation of ' Devereux, or P. Clifford, or E. Aram, Esquires' ; and the moral of the tale is ' that Homicide is not to be permitted even to the most amiable Genius.' The dramatic effectiveness of the original was, on the other hand, distinctly perceptible in an amusing extravaganza produced at the Adelphi some thirty or forty years since. Some playgoers of the past besides myself may remember the inimitable agility with which in this piece Mr. Toole skipped over the counter, and the strength of passion which that gifted actress Miss Woolgar (Mrs. Alfred Mellon) put into the part of Millwood. The ' Travestie ' of the story of *George Barnwell* in *Rejected Addresses* (one of the contributions of ' Momus Medlar '), though included in Jeffrey's praise of being ' as good as that sort of thing can be,' is one of the few things in the famous volume whose wit will not keep them fresh.

[2] From a copy of Genest, with MSS. notes, bequeathed to the British Museum in 1844 by Mr. Frederick Latreille, vol. III, p. 488, note.

[3] *London Daily Post*, Thursday, May 7, 1736.

has been seen, was a steady admirer and friend of Lillo) with his *Pasquin, a Dramatick Satire on the Times.* Thomas Davies, the dramatist's future editor, as well as author of a *Life of Garrick* and of *Dramatic Miscellanies,* took the part of young Wilmot. He says that the play was not successful at first, but that Fielding afterwards tacked it to his *Historical Register* (which had so signal, though short-lived, a *succès de scandale*), and that it was then performed to more advantage and often repeated. It was reproduced at the Haymarket in 1755 with a Prologue by the younger Cibber,[1] which seems never to have been printed ; and again, at the same theatre, by the elder Colman in 1782.[2] Colman, besides adding a new Prologue, introduced some alterations which, without affecting the general course or texture of the piece, were considerable as well as, on the whole, judicious. Their nature will be apparent from the following remarks, which form the earlier portion of the *Postscript* appended by Colman, with his signature and the date ' Soho-Square, June 28, 1783,' to his edition of the play, published in 1783:[3]

' Though the *Fatal Curiosity* of LILLO has received the applause of many sound critics, and been accounted

[1] So Genest says, IV, 425. The advertisement of the play in the daily papers of September 4, 1755, runs : ' With ORIGINAL Prologue, spoken by Cibber's.'

[2] It was the *younger* Colman who brought out, in 1798, a ' dramatic romance,' called *Bluebeard, or Female Curiosity.*

[3] For these changes see the footnotes to the text in the present volume. The remainder of the *Postscript,* with the exception of its concluding sentence, is reprinted in Appendix II : *The Source of Fatal Curiosity.*

worthy of the Graecian stage, and (what is, perhaps, still
higher merit) worthy of Shakespeare! yet the long ex-
clusion of this drama from the theatre had in some measure obscured the fame of a tragedy, whose uncommon
excellence challenged more celebrity. The late Mr. Harris, of Salisbury,[1] has endeavoured, in his PHILOLOGICAL
INQUIRIES, to display the beauties, *the terrible graces*, of
the piece, and to do justice to the memory of LILLO.
His comment is in general just, yet he seems to have
given a sketch of *the Fable* from an imperfect recollection
of the circumstances, without the book before him. He
appears to have conceived that the tragedy derived its
title from the *curiosity* of Agnes to know the contents of
the casket : but that LILLO meant to mark by the title
the FATAL CURIOSITY of Young Wilmot, is evident
from the whole scene between him and Randal, wherein
he arranges the plan of his intended interview with his
parents ; which arrangement Mr. Harris erroneously at-
tributes to his conference with Charlot. The principle of
CURIOSITY is openly avowed and warmly sustained by
Young Wilmot, and humbly reprehended by Randal.

'The comment of Mr. Harris is, however, on the
whole, most judicious and liberal. It concludes with a
note in these words:

' "If any one read this tragedy, the author of these
Inquiries has a request or two to make, for which he
hopes a candid reader will forgive him — One is, not to
cavil at minute in-accuracies, but [to] look to the superior
merit of *the whole taken together*. — Another is, totally

---

[1] James Harris, author of *Hermes*, and father of the first Earl of
Malmesbury. Harris was carried away by his admiration of *Fatal
Curiosity*, which he compares, on an equal footing, to the *Œdipus
Tyrannus* in the conception and arrangement of the fable, and which
he subsequently extols for its ' insistency of manners.'

to expunge those wretched *rhimes*, which conclude many of the scenes ; and which, 't is probable, are not from Lillo, but from some other hand, willing to conform to an absurd fashion, *then* practised, but now laid aside, the fashion (I mean) of a *rhiming conclusion.*" *Philological Inquiries,* vol. 1, p. 174.

' The present Editor thought it his duty to remove, as far as he was able, the blemishes here noticed by Mr. Harris ; and he therefore expunged *the rhiming conclusions* of acts and scenes, except in one instance, where he thought the couplet too beautiful to be displaced. Some *minute inaccuracies* of language he also hazarded an attempt to correct ; and even in some measure to mitigate the horror of the catastrophe, by the omission of some expressions rather too savage, and by one or two touches of remorse and tenderness. Agnes is most happily drawn after Lady Macbeth ; in whose character there is not perhaps a finer trait, than her saying, during the murder of Duncan,

> " Had he not resembled
> My father as he slept, I had done't ! " ' [1]

The play was reproduced by the elder Colman at the same theatre in 1782. In 1784 an alteration of the play by Henry Mackenzie, author of *The Man of Feeling*, was performed — once only — at Covent Garden, under the title of *The Shipwreck*. This version is in five acts, and introduces a boy Charles, grandson to Agnes, who unnecessarily complicates the action. [2] Finally, it was revived in 1813 at Bath under

---

[1] The above fails to exhaust the bare-faced plagiarisms from *Macbeth* in the murder-scene in Lillo's play.

[2] Genest, VIII, 310, does not mention Charles, who appears in Acts II, III, and V, where there is a good deal about him. Agnes

the title of *The Cornish Shipwreck, or Fatal Curiosity,*
when an additional scene was performed, in which
young Wilmot appears after he has been stabbed, and
in a dying state. This scene, which is said to have
been by Lillo's hand, although it is not printed in any
extant edition, and which had been presented to the
less sensitive Bristol public without giving rise to any
dissatisfaction, now provoked so much disturbance that
the curtain had to drop.[1]

In the *Postscript* already cited Colman narrates the
episode which suggested to Lillo the plot of his tragedy, and mentions his belief that the story was no
longer extant except in Frankland's *Annals of the Reigns
of King James and King Charles the First*.[2] He
adds a reference to the *Biographia Dramatica,* in
which the source of the story is stated to be a black-
letter pamphlet of 1618 entitled *News from Perin in
Cornwall,* etc. But before Frankland, the story had
been reproduced from the pamphlet by W. Sanderson's
Compleat History of the Lives and Reigns of Mary,

does not reveal whether he is the son of her son or of a daughter,
though she says that his mother is dead. For an account by Mackenzie of the motives for his changes see *Biographia Dramatica,* vol.
III (ed. 1812), under *The Shipwreck.* They show, as might be
expected, a higher degree of refinement than seems to have been
thought necessary by the theatrical public ; but they are neverthe-
less finely conceived.

   1 Genest, VIII, 388.

   2 [Dr. Thomas Frankland's] *The Annals of King James and
King Charles the First both of happy memory* (from 1612–1642),
London, 1681, fol. ser. p. 33, where this ' calamity of wondrous
note ' is said to have happened at ' Perinin ' in Cornwall, in September, 1618, and where the story is told immediately after the
account of the death of Sir Walter Ralegh.

Queen of Scotland, and of her Son and Successor James.
(London, 1656, pp. 463–65.)[1] Indeed, I find that
the entire reign of James as given in Frankland is, except
for insignificant changes, a mere reproduction of Sanderson's account, and that the story of the murder is virtu-
ally identical in the two histories. As in Frankland, the
story in Sanderson follows immediately the account of
the death of Sir Walter Ralegh. A copy of the pamphlet
is preserved in the Bodleian at Oxford; and I have availed
myself of the kind permission of the Bodleian authorities
and the courtesy of Mr. George Parker to reproduce the
original *in extenso* in an Appendix for comparison with
the Frankland-Sanderson version and the play itself. I
have there also mentioned some of the *analoga* to the
story which have been noted by earlier and more recent
research. It will not escape observation that in the
pamphlet, where the story has a long and elaborate
exordium, the instigator of the crime is the step-mother,
not the mother, of its victim ; but that Frankland, or
rather his original, Sanderson, — and one of these accounts was probably that used by Lillo, — deepens the
horror of the deed by ascribing it to the mother.

[1] Noted by Reinhard Köhler, *Ueber den Stoff von Zacharias
Werner's Vierundzwanzigsten Februar* (*Kleinere Schriften* &c.,
hrsgbn. von I. Bolte, Berlin, 1900, vol. III, pp. 185–199) — an
exhaustive essay very kindly pointed out to me by Professor Erich
Schmidt — who cites G. C. Boase and W. P. Courtney, *Biblio-
theca Cornubiensis* (1874), vol. I, p. 319. Frankland's version is also
to be found in Baker's *Biographia Dramatica* (ed. 1812), vol. II,
pp. 224–261. There are several later references to the story. See
also W. E. A. Axon, *The Story of Fatal Curiosity* in *Notes and
Queries*, 6 ser. 5, 21 f. (1882).

The time, then, at which the action of *Fatal Curiosity*
is laid, is the latter part of the reign of James I, after
Sir Walter Ralegh's last return from Guiana in 1618;
but the dramatist evidently takes into account the strong
feeling against Spain which prevailed in England about
the time of the production of this tragedy. Two years
later — in 1738 — this state of feeling was to be increased to a pitch of frenzy by the story of Jenkins's
ear; and in the following year Walpole was con-
strained to declare war against Spain. The scene of
the action is Penrhyn (near Falmouth), in Cornwall, which at one time enjoyed the reputation of
being the smallest borough in England, but which
still returns a member to Parliament. Lillo seems to
have little or no acquaintance with the place,¹ but to
have taken some interest in the misdeeds of the Cornish wreckers, of which, in the last scene of the first act
of this play, he speaks with grave reprobation, as a
scandal that ought to be ended. As a matter of fact
an act of great severity had been passed against this evil
in the reign of Queen Anne, and made perpetual under
George I; but when Wesley visited Cornwall in 1776,
he found that this 'especial scandal' of the country, as
Mr. Lecky calls it, was still as common there as ever.²

¹ In the first scene of the play Randal says:

' I saw her pass the High-Street t'wards the minster.'

The noble parish-church of St. Gluvias (with its interesting mon-
uments of the Pendarves family and others) can at no time have been
called 'the minster.' It is about a mile away from the High Street.

² Lecky's *History of England in the Eighteenth Century* (2d ed.)
489. Cf. the reference to the 'inhospitable ways' of these folk
in *The London Merchant*, Act IV, *ad fin.*

It should be noted that, unlike *The London Merchant,* this play is throughout written in blank verse, a circumstance in accord with the general character of the diction, which has a tendency to be more ornate than that of the earlier work. The blank verse is, however, by no means excellent of its kind, and, curiously enough, is at times less smooth than so much of the prose of *The London Merchant* as runs into metre. Lillo has a habit of prefixing a redundant syllable to a six-foot line ; but, even allowing for this, his lines do not always run easily. Thus we have in the opening scene :

> ' *Whose* perfection ends in knowing we know nothing.'
> ' *Is* tir'd or exhausted — curst condition ! '

His elisions too are often harsh, as :

> ' *By* unjust suspicion I know the truth.

Colman, in his revised edition, showed his good taste by ' expunging the rhyming conclusions of acts and scenes.'

There can be no doubt that, as Colman pointed out, the title of *Fatal Curiosity* contains no reference, as might be supposed, — or, at all events, that it does not refer primarily, — to the ' curiosity ' of Mrs. Wilmot (Agnes) in opening the casket brought into his parents' house by their unknown son.[1] It refers in the first instance to the ' curiosity ' — a kind of ὕβρις or presumption on his good fortune — displayed by Young Wilmot, when he tempts Providence in order to se-

---

[1] In the opening speech of Act III, Agnes says :

> ' Why should my *curiosity* excite me
> To search and pry into th' affairs of others ? '

cure to himself a certain heightening or *raffinement*
of enjoyment by visiting his parents without having
first discovered himself to them. As to this the expressions of Young Wilmot and the faithful Randal before
the commission of the error [1] and the reflexion of the
former after he has committed it,[2] leave no room for
doubt.

The interest attaching to *Fatal Curiosity* in connexion with the general course of dramatic literature lies
in the fact of its being an early experiment in a species
to which the Germans, who alone cultivated it to any
considerable extent, have given the name of *Schicksalstragödie* — the tragedy of destiny. This species must
be regarded, not as introducing a new element into
tragic action, but as exaggerating in various degrees of
grotesqueness (I here use the word ' grotesque ' in its
proper, which is also very close to its etymological,
meaning) an element which in itself is foreign neither to
ancient nor to modern tragedy. Professor Lewis Camp-

---

[1] In the scene between Young Wilmot and Randal in Act II
the former asks :

> ' Why may I not
> Indulge my *curiosity* and try
> If it be possible by seeing first
> My parents as a stranger, to improve
> This pleasure by surprise ? '

and Randal replies :

> ' You grow luxurious in mental pleasures ;
> . . . To say true, I ever thought
> Your boundless *curiosity* a weakness.'

[2] Act II, *ad fin.*, Young Wilmot exclaims :

> ' How has my *curiosity* betray'd me
> Into superfluous pain ! I faint with fondness,
> And shall, if I stay longer, rush upon 'em,' etc.

bell, in a work from which I have already quoted, has a passage on this subject at once so pertinent and so judicious that I cannot refrain from giving it in full :

'As Mr. W. L. Courtney puts it, "tragedy is always a clash of two powers — necessity without, freedom within ; outside, a great, rigid, arbitrary law of fate ; inside, the moderated individual will, which can win its spiritual triumphs even when all its material surroundings and environment have crumbled into hopeless ruin. . . . Necessity without, liberty within — that is the great theme which, however disguised, runs through every tragedy that has been written in the world." But it is commonly assumed that, whereas in Æschylus and Sophocles the necessity is wholly outward, in Shakespeare it is the direct outcome of personality ; that while the theme of ancient drama is, as Wordsworth says,

> "Poor humanity's afflicted will
>   Struggling in vain with ruthless destiny,"

in Shakespeare the tragic hero is encountered by the consequences of his own errors, so that here, far more than in the Greek masterpieces, we see exemplified the truth of the Greek proverb "Character is destiny"; "no fate broods over the actions of men and the history of families; the only fatality is the fatality of character." (*Dowden.*)

'This is only partly true. All ancient art and thought is in its form more objective, while an ever-growing subjectivity is the note of the modern mind ; and the ancient fables mostly turned on some predetermined fatality. But in his moulding of the fable the Attic poet was guided by his own profound conception of human nature as he saw it in its freest working. The idea of fate is thus, as it were,

expanded into an outer framework for the picture of life,
except in so far as it remains to symbolize those inscrutable
causes beyond human control, whose working is likewise
present to the mind of Shakespeare. Xerxes, Agamem-
non, Clytemnestra, Ajax, Creon are no less victims of
their own passionate nature than Macbeth or Lear ; and
the fate of Hamlet almost equally with that of Œdipus is
due to antecedent and surrounding circumstances with
which neither he nor any man could have power to cope ;
although here also malign fortune is assisted by "the o'er-
growth of some complexion, Oft breaking down the pales
and forts of reason." ' [1]

I have cited this passage as it stands ; but I cannot
conceal my opinion that more lurks in the reservation
' *almost equally* ' in its concluding sentence than might
perhaps be obvious at first sight. There is a provoca-
tion of character in *Œdipus* as in *Hamlet ;* but Hamlet
is, and Œdipus is not, pitted on equal terms against the
power of fate ; and the mighty Sophoclean trilogy must
remain, as Vischer puts it, the most signal instance of
the inability of Greek tragedy to solve the problem of the
conflict between destiny and guilt. [2]

But in any case Lillo, whether consciously or not,
in his *Fatal Curiosity* took a step which may be re-

---

[1] L. Campbell, *Tragic Drama in Aeschylus, etc.*, pp. 29-31.

[2] See the powerful passage in F. T. Vischer's *Æsthetik oder
Wissenschaft des Schönen*, part iii, section ii, p. 1410 (vol. iv
of 1857 ed.). I much regret to be unable to refer to a paper by
the late Professor H. T. Rötscher, *Zufall und Nothwendigkeit im
Drama* in *Jahrbücher für dramatische Kunst und Literatur.* (It
is not in *Jahrgang* 1848, as I have at last, to my great disappointment, ascertained.)

garded as transnormal : not because in the narrow
framework of his domestic tragedy he once more pic-
tured *la fuerza del destino* — the force of destiny —
which few tragic dramatists, great or small, have pretended to ignore, but because, in point of fact, he ex-
hibited destiny as operating to all intents and purposes
independently of character. The demoralising effects
of want and ' dire necessity ' upon Old Wilmot and
his wife are of course quite insufficient to account for
the sophistry with which she ' seduces his will ' and
' infects his soul ' so as to secure his connivance in her
criminal design. On the other hand, the ' curiosity '
of their son in taking them unawares, which the author
wishes us to accept as the really fatal starting-point in
the series of events that end in the catastrophe of both
son and parents, is, if a weakness, a perfectly natural
and pardonable one. The effect of this tragedy is
therefore as hollow as it is horrible ; like Quarles' *Emblem* of the vacuous world, *tinnit, inane est ;* and it
appropriately ends with the twofold commonplace, that
the ways of heaven are mysterious, and that

> ' The ripe in virtue never die too soon.'

We know that Lillo's tragedy found its way to Germany, where, after, in 1781, — the year before that in
which he started on his well-known journey to England,
— Karl Philipp Moritz had produced a genuine imitation
of *Fatal Curiosity*,[1] two editions were published of a
not very happily named translation of it by W. H.

---

[1] *Blunt oder der Gast.* Schauspiel in einem Akt. Berlin, 1781.

Brömel, *Stolz und Verzweiflung* (*Pride and Despair*).[1]
In the same country a great dramatic poet was about
this time, with much searching of soul and a lofty desire
to realise the truest and most enduring conceptions of
tragedy and her laws, seeking to apply the idea of Fate
exemplified in the Attic drama to his own practice.[2]
Already in his great *Wallenstein* trilogy, where the
association of the subject with a period and a hero of
well-known astrological propensities would in any case
have led to the introduction of a fatalistic element,
Schiller endeavoured to reconcile this with the higher
or moral law to which the universe is subject.[3] And
The Bride of Messina, the beautiful play which, perhaps not altogether successfully, he sought to model on

---

[1] Dessau and Leipzig, 1785 ; and Augsburg, 1791.

[2] For what follows cf. Professor Jakob Minor's general and special Introductions to a selection of plays by Z. Werner, Müllner
and Houwald, published under the title *Das Schicksalsdrama* in the
Deutsche National-Literatur series edited by J. Kürschner (Berlin
and Stuttgart, W. Spemann) and Dr. Minor's larger work, *Die
Schicksalstragödie in ihren Hauptvertretern* (Frankfort, 1883).

[3] Compare Wallenstein's famous narrative, justifying his confidence in Octavio, in *The Piccolomini*, Act v, Sc. 4, beginning
(in Coleridge's Translation),

'There exist moments in the life of man,' &c.,

and the Duke's comment, in reply to Illo,

'There's no such thing as chance'—

with the magnificent passage in *The Death of Wallenstein*, Act i,
Sc. 9, when he discovers that Octavio has played traitor to him :

'The stars lie not; but we have here a work
Wrought counter to the stars and destiny.
The science still is honest ; this false heart
Forces a lie on the truth-telling heaven.
On a divine law divination rests,' &c.

Attic examples, concludes with lines that in their native form have become proverbial :

> ' Of man's possessions life is not the highest,
>   But of all ills on earth the worst is guilt.'

Far different were the conceptions and the practice on this head of a school of dramatists who, while striving more or less to imitate Schiller both in the treatment of their themes and in the outer form of their plays, found it expedient to fall back into narrower tracks of their own. Their notion of fate was an elaborately artificial system of predestination which, as it were, set out to entangle its victims, like a *mouchard* luring a *suspect* step by step to the perpetration of the cardinal deed. The working of this system depended on coincidences of time and place, on recurring dates of day and month, on the occasion offered by inanimate things, on the premonition received from inarticulate sounds, on the accidents of accidents.[1] Some of these poets were trained lawyers, and all seem to have had a taste, natural or acquired, for stories of parricide and incest, ' odious involutions and perversions of passion,' to cite an admirable expression of Sir Walter Scott's,[2] — the whole paraphernalia of the criminal novel and the police newspaper. Of course their methods differed in degree according to their daring, and in effectiveness according to their literary and theatrical ability ; for

[1] Everything, says a character in Müllner's *Schüld* (Act IV, Sc. 4), in the end depends on the silver *real* which my mother refused to a beggar-woman.

[2] *Letters and Recollections of Sir Walter Scott.* By Mrs. Hughes (of Uffington). Edited by H. G. Hutchinson. London, 1904.

there was among them more than one man of genius and more than one born playwright. Their metrical form, preferentially short trochaic lines with irregular rhymes, was happily chosen; for it was at once insinuating and uncomfortable; and it was at times managed with very notable skill.

The same story as that which forms the subject of *Fatal Curiosity* furnished the plot of the one-act tragedy of *Der Vierundzwanzigste Februar*, by Zacharias Werner, a gifted writer of ephemeral celebrity, but unmistakable talent. This play (1812), of which the scene is laid in a solitary inn in a rocky Alpine pass, is much more firmly constructed and much more overpowering in its effect than *Fatal Curiosity;* nor can it be denied that the piece has a certain passionate force which smacks of genius. But after one is relieved of the *incubus*, there remains little to impress the mind in connexion with this play, except the fact that Goethe allowed it to be produced on the Weimar stage.[1] While Werner's

---

[1] According to a Weimar tradition, corroborated by Werner's account to Iffland that a 'well-known' anecdote supplied the foundation of his play, an incident, read out at Goethe's house in 1809, was recommended by him to Werner as a subject for a one-act tragedy. The relations between Goethe and Werner have been recently illustrated by their correspondence published with an interesting introduction by MM. O. Schüddekopf and O. Walzel in *Goethe und die Romantik*, vol. II (*Schriften der Goethe Gesellschaft*, vol. XIV. Weimar, 1899). It may be added that in 1808 Prince Pückler-Muskau heard at Geneva of a similar occurrence in the vicinity; and that early in June, 1880, there appeared in the *Neue Freie Presse* of Vienna a story to the same intent (the mother being, however, the sole agent), which ran its course through the journals of both hemispheres (see Axon, *u. s.*).

tragedy must in one sense be called original, Adolf Müllner's one-act tragedy, which deals with a similar theme and frankly calls itself *Der Neunundzwanzigste Februar* (*February the twenty-ninth*) (also 1812), is a palpable attempt at outdoing the sensation excited by its predecessor. Here, to the accompaniment of atmospheric effects, *sortes biblicae*, and the actual grinding of the knife destined to cut the unspeakable knot, a tale is unfolded which need not fear the competition of the most complex of nightmares. Yet so alive were Müllner's theatrical instincts to the public sentiment, that he afterwards skilfully changed the action of this play of horrors into one with a 'happy ending' (*Der Wahn — The Illusion*). The same author's celebrated four-act tragedy *Die Schuld* (*Guilt*), produced in the same year 1812, marked the height of the vogue reached by the 'Tragedy of Destiny'; for its popularity at Vienna and elsewhere knew no bounds. The scene of this play is laid on the North Sea coast of the Scandinavian peninsula; but the chief characters in the action are Spaniards — a daring but felicitous combination. The complicated story of crime and its sequel is no doubt worked out with the skill of a *virtuoso*; and from the snapping of a chord of the hysterical Elvira's harp during her opening speech onwards a continuous sense of unconquerable gloom possesses the spectator; nor does it release him with the closing oracular announcement, that the *pourquoi* of the *pourquoi* (to borrow the Electress Sophia's phrase) will not be revealed till the day of the Resurrection.

There can be no doubt that the eminent Austrian

dramatist, Franz Grillparzer, who afterward came near to
greatness in more legitimate fields of tragic composition,
was in some measure inspired by Müllner's *Die Schuld*
in the production of his *Die Ahnfrau* (*The Ancestress*) in
1817; although he seems justified in his vehement protest that this play was not properly speaking a tragedy
of destiny, but one in which wrong is visited where the
responsibility has been incurred. But the species itself
lingered on for something like a decade more, without
being killed either by academic or farcical ridicule.[1] But
nothing of any importance was produced in the later
stages of this literary mode. The last in any way conspicuous production of the kind was Baron C. E. von
Houwald's *Der Leuchtthurm* (*The Lighthouse*), a
rather mawkish play, that makes large use of natural
phenomena — the howling winds and the surging waves
— which Lillo had not ignored, but introduced with less
sentimental profusion, when he made a shipwreck on
the unkind Cornish coast the pivot of the action of his
Fatal Curiosity.

As a dramatist Lillo was distinguished by no mean
constructive power, by a naturalness of diction capable
of becoming ardent without bombast, and of remaining

---

[1] A list of these plays and of one or two parodies upon the species will be found in Goedeke's *Grundriss der deutschen Dichtung,*
vol. III, pp. 381–84. It would carry me too far to discuss here
Platen's memorable attack on the *Schicksalstragödie,* among other
aberrations of contemporary literature from his classical ideals, in *Die
Verhängnissvolle Gabel* (*The Fatal Fork*), 1826, and *Der roman-
tische Œdipus* (*The Romantic Œdipus*), 1829. Among the flies
caught in the amber of Platen's verse, these at least were not quite
ephemerae.

plain without sinking into baldness, and by a gift, con-
spicuously exercised in the earlier of the two plays here
presented and to some extent also in the later, of re-
producing genuine types of human nature alive with
emotion and passion. In dramatic history he is notable
rather because of the effects of his chief works than
because of those works themselves. *The London Merchant*, which alone entitles him to an enduring fame,
is true to the genius of the English drama. Thus while
our own theatre, in a period of much artificiality, owed
to him a strengthening of its tie with real life and
its experiences, his revival of domestic tragedy both
directly and indirectly quickened the general course of
dramatic literature, expanded its choice of themes, and
suggested a manner of treatment most itself when nearest the language of the heart.

A. W. WARD.

PETERHOUSE LODGE, CAMBRIDGE, ENGLAND,
    November, 1905.

THE TEXT

The text of *The London Merchant* is printed from the first edition, 1731. It has been collated with the second (1731), fourth (1732), and seventh (1740) octavo editions, and the two collective editions by Davies, 1775 and 1810. O2 is identically the same as O1, except that it has "Second Edition" on the title-page, above "London," and in Scene XII of Act V corrects *unalterable* to *unutterable*. O4 much improves on O1, but O7 is little more than a reprint of O4, with some errors of its own. The exception is its addition of Scene XI of Act V, which probably first appeared in O5. Prolonged inquiry has not revealed any copy of O3, O5, or O6. In O4 the French division of the scenes used in O1 and O2 is changed to the English method. As the 1775 edition does little more than reprint O7, and the 1810 edition closely follows O1, in the variants only departures of these late editions from their originals are noted.

In accordance with the custom of the series, evident errors have been silently corrected, and punctuation and capitalization modernized. Change has been needed in Lillo's punctuation, for his avoidance of the difficulties of punctuation by a very free use of dashes gave an unnecessarily hysterical effect to a play already tense enough, and even at times led to confusion of the thought. When any variation from the reading of O1 has been admitted, the original reading has been noted in the variants at the foot of the page. *Aside*, and similar directions, standing at the end of a line or speech, have been silently transferred to the beginning. The text of Scene XI, Act V, has been taken from O7, the first accessible edition containing it. Use of O4 has been possible through the courtesy of the Library of Yale University.

THE
London Merchant:
OR, THE
HISTORY
OF
GEORGE BARNWELL.

As it is Acted at the

THEATRE-ROYAL
IN
DRURY-LANE.

By HIS MAJESTY's Servants.

By Mr. *LILLO.*

Learn to be wise from others Harm,
And you shall do full well.
Old Ballad of the Lady's Fall.

LONDON:
Printed for J. GRAY, at the *Cross-Keys* in the *Poultry*; and
sold by J. ROBERTS, in *Warwick-Lane.* MDCCXXXI.

[Price One Shilling and Six-pence.]

SOURCES

The story of *The London Merchant* was manifestly suggested to Lillo by the old ballad, which is to be found in Bishop Percy's *Reliques of Ancient English Poetry* and in *English and Scottish Ballads*, selected and edited by F. J. Child. From the latter it is here reprinted as an appendix. While there is a general agreement between ballad and play, the former contains nothing as to the virtuous attachment of the master's daughter for Barnwell, or as to the friendship of his fellow apprentice; and, with regard to Barnwell himself, the story in the ballad takes a different close, sending him out to meet his fate 'in Polonia,' instead of bringing him to justice in company with his paramour at home. Probably Lillo had access to some source or sources of information concerning the story of George Barnwell besides the old ballad itself. A novel, *Barnwell*, circa 1796, by T. S. Surr, deviates from the facts even more than Lillo's play. Possibly Lillo made use of the same sources as the author of *Memoirs of George Barnwell, the unhappy subject of Lillo's celebrated Tragedy, derived from the most authentic source, and intended for the perusal and instruction of the Rising Generation. By a Descendant of the Barnwell Family.* Printed at Harlow [in Essex] by B. Flower for W. Jones . . . of No. 5, Newgate Street, London, 1810. For a discussion of the sources of the play see *Introduction*, pp. xvi–xx.

TO

Sir JOHN EYLES, *Bar*.

MEMBER OF PARLIAMENT FOR, AND ALDER-
MAN OF THE CITY OF *London*, AND SUB-
GOVERNOR OF THE *South-Sea* COMPANY.

SIR,

If Tragick Poetry be, as Mr. *Dryden* has some where
said, the most excellent and most useful kind of writing,
the more extensively useful the moral of any tragedy is,
the more excellent that piece must be of its kind.

I hope I shall not be thought to insinuate that this, to   5
which I have presumed to prefix your name, is such;
that depends on its fitness to answer the end of tragedy,
the exciting of the passions, in order to the correcting
such of them as are criminal, either in their nature, or
through their excess. Whether the following scenes do   10
this in any tolerable degree, is, with the deference that
becomes one who wou'd not be thought vain, submitted
to your candid and impartial judgment.

What I wou'd infer is this, I think, evident truth;
that tragedy is so far from losing its dignity, by being   15

To Sir John Eyles. The dedicatory essay is not given in O7, though it
appears in all other editions that have been accessible.

accommodated to the circumstances of the generality of mankind, that it is more truly august in proportion to the extent of its influence, and the numbers that are properly affected by it. As it is more truly great to be the instrument of good to many, who stand in need of our assistance, than to a very small part of that number.

If Princes, &c. were alone liable to misfortunes, arising from vice, or weakness in themselves or others, there wou'd be good reason for confining the characters in tragedy to those of superior rank ; but, since the contrary is evident, nothing can be more reasonable than to proportion the remedy to the disease.

I am far from denying that tragedies, founded on any instructive and extraordinary events in history, or a well-invented fable, where the persons introduced are of the highest rank, are without their use, even to the bulk of the audience. The strong contrast between a *Tamerlane* and a *Bajazet*, may have its weight with an unsteady people, and contribute to the fixing of them in the interest of a Prince of the character of the former, when, thro' their own levity, or the arts of designing men, they are render'd factious and uneasy, tho' they have the highest reason to be satisfied. The sentiments and example of a *Cato*, may inspire his spectators with a just sense of the value of liberty, when they see that honest patriot prefer death to an obligation from a tyrant, who wou'd sacrifice the constitution of his country, and the liberties of mankind, to his ambition or revenge. I have attempted,

29-30 *or a . . . fable.* O4, 1775, print, fables ; 1810 omits *a.*

indeed, to enlarge the province of the graver kind of
poetry, and should be glad to see it carried on by some   45
abler hand. Plays founded on moral tales in private life
may be of admirable use, by carrying conviction to the
mind with such irresistible force as to engage all the faculties and powers of the soul in the cause of virtue, by
stifling vice in its first principles. They who imagine   50
this to be too much to be attributed to tragedy, must be
strangers to the energy of that noble species of poetry.
Shakespear, who has given such amazing proofs of his
genius, in that as well as in comedy, in his *Hamlet* has
the following lines :   55

> *Had he the motive and the cause for passion*
> *That I have, he wou'd drown the stage with tears*
> *And cleave the general ear with horrid speech ;*
> *Make mad the guilty, and appal the free,*
> *Confound the ignorant ; and amaze indeed*   60
> *The very faculty of eyes and ears.*

And farther, in the same speech :

> *I 've heard that guilty creatures at a play*
> *Have, by the very cunning of the scene,*
> *Been so struck to the soul, that presently*   65
> *They have proclaim'd their malefactions.*

Prodigious ! yet strictly just. But I shan't take up
your valuable time with my remarks ; only give me

---

63 *I've heard . . . play.* 1810, more correctly :
                      . . . I have heard,
         . . . That guilty creatures sitting at a play.
65 *so struck.* 1810, struck so.
67 *shan't.* 1775, 1810, shall not.

leave just to observe, that he seems so firmly perswaded of the power of a well wrote piece to produce the effect here ascribed to it, as to make *Hamlet* venture his soul on the event, and rather trust that than a messenger from the other world, tho' it assumed, as he expresses it, his noble father's form, and assured him that it was his spirit. "I 'll have," says *Hamlet*, "grounds more relative " ;

> . . . *The Play 's the thing,*
> *Wherein I 'll catch the conscience of the King.*

Such plays are the best answers to them who deny the lawfulness of the stage.

Considering the novelty of this attempt, I thought it would be expected from me to say something in its excuse ; and I was unwilling to lose the opportunity of saying something of the usefulness of Tragedy in general, and what may be reasonably expected from the farther improvement of this excellent kind of poetry.

Sir, I hope you will not think I have said too much of an art, a mean specimen of which I am ambitious enough to recommend to your favour and protection. A mind, conscious of superior worth, as much despises flattery, as it is above it. Had I found in my self an inclination to so contemptible a vice, I should not have chose Sir JOHN EYLES for my patron. And indeed the best writ panegyrick, tho' strictly true, must place you in a light much inferior to that in which you have long been fix'd by the love and esteem of your fellow citizens ;

whose choice of you for one of their representatives in Parliament has sufficiently declared their sense of your merit. Nor hath the knowledge of your worth been confined to the City. The Proprietors in the *South-Sea* 100 Company, in which are included numbers of persons as considerable for their rank, fortune, and understanding, as any in the Kingdom, gave the greatest proof of their confidence in your capacity and probity, when they chose you Sub-Governor of their Company, at a time when 105 their affairs were in the utmost confusion, and their properties in the greatest danger. Nor is the Court insensible of your importance. I shall not therefore attempt your character, nor pretend to add any thing to a reputation so well established.   110

Whatever others may think of a Dedication wherein there is so much said of other things, and so little of the person to whom it is address'd, I have reason to believe that you will the more easily pardon it on that very account.   115

> I am, SIR,
> Your most obedient
> humble servant,
> GEORGE LILLO.

107 *Nor.* O4, Neither.

PROLOGUE.

Spoke by Mr. CIBBER, *Jun.*

The Tragick Muse, sublime, delights to show
Princes distrest and scenes of royal woe;
In awful pomp, majestick, to relate
The fall of nations or some heroe's fate;
That scepter'd chiefs may by example know   5
The strange vicissitude of things below:
What dangers on security attend;
How pride and cruelty in ruin end;
Hence Providence supream to know, and own
Humanity adds glory to a throne.   10
  In ev'ry former age and foreign tongue
With native grandure thus the Goddess sung.
Upon our stage indeed, with wish'd success,
You've sometimes seen her in a humbler dress —
Great only in distress. When she complains   15
In Southern's, Rowe's, *or* Otway's *moving strains,*
The brilliant drops that fall from each bright eye
The absent pomp with brighter jems supply.
Forgive us then, if we attempt to show,
In artless strains, a tale of private woe.   20
A London '*Prentice ruin'd is our theme,*
Drawn from the fam'd old song that bears his name.

Spoke. O7, Spoken.   14 *a humbler.* O7, an humbler.

We hope your taste is not so high to scorn
A moral tale, esteem'd e'er you were born;
Which, for a century of rolling years,   25
Has fill'd a thousand-thousand eyes with tears.
If thoughtless youth to warn, and shame the age
From vice destructive, well becomes the stage;
If this example innocence secure,
Prevent our guilt, or by reflection cure;   30
If Millwood's *dreadful guilt and sad despair*
Commend the virtue of the good and fair:
Tho' art be wanting, and our numbers fail,
Indulge th' attempt in justice to the tale!

    29 *secure.* O4, O7, insure.
    30 *Prevent,* O4, O7, 1810. O1, Prevents.
    31 *guilt.* O4, O7, crimes.
    34 *th'.* O7, the.

DRAMATIS PERSONAE.

MEN.

Thorowgood, ... Mr. *Bridgwater*.
Barnwell, *Uncle to* George, . . Mr. *Roberts*.
George Barnwell, . . . Mr. *Cibber*, Jun.
Trueman, ... Mr. *W. Mills*.
Blunt, ... Mr. *R. Wetherilt*.
[Jailer.
John.]

WOMEN.

Maria, ... Mrs. *Cibber*.
Millwood, ... Mrs. *Butler*.
Lucy, ... Mrs. *Charke*.
Officers with their Attendants, Keeper, and Footmen.

SCENE, London, *and an adjacent Village.*

Wetherilt. O4, Witherhilt ; 1775, Witherhile : both incorrectly.
Millwood. So all the editions, and throughout the play.
Blunt. 1775 and 1810 add: Jailer. John.
Charke. 1775 and 1810, incorrectly, Clarke.
Lucy. O7, Lucia.

The
London Merchant
or the
History
of
George Barnwell

Act I.

Scene I. *A Room in Thorowgood's House.*

[Enter] Thorowgood and Trueman.

Trueman. Sir, the packet from Genoa is arriv'd. *Gives letters.*

Thorowgood. Heav'n be praised, the storm that threaten'd our royal mistress, pure religion, liberty and laws, is for a time diverted; the haughty and revengeful Spaniard, disappointed of the loan on which he depended from Genoa, must now attend the slow return of wealth from his

5

Act I. Scene I. Of the editions examined (see Note on Texts) only O1 and O2 use the French method of dividing the scenes.

new world, to supply his empty coffers, e'er he
can execute his purpos'd invasion of our happy 10
island; by which means time is gain'd to make
such preparations on our part as may, Heav'n
concurring, prevent his malice, or turn the medi-
tated mischief on himself.

True. He must be insensible indeed, who is 15
not affected when the safety of his country is
concern'd.—Sir, may I know by what means—
if I am too bold—

Thor. Your curiosity is laudable; and I grat-
ify it with the greater pleasure, because from 20
thence you may learn how honest merchants,
as such, may sometimes contribute to the safety
of their country, as they do at all times to its happiness; that if hereafter you should be tempted
to any action that has the appearance of vice or 25
meanness in it, upon reflecting on the dignity of
our profession, you may with honest scorn reject
whatever is unworthy of it.

True. Shou'd Barnwell, or I, who have the
benefit of your example, by our ill conduct 30
bring any imputation on that honourable name,
we must be left without excuse.

Thor. You complement, young man. (*Trueman bows respectfully.*) Nay, I'm not offended.
As the name of merchant never degrades the 35
gentleman, so by no means does it exclude him;

only take heed not to purchase the character of
complaisant at the expence of your sincerity. —
But to answer your question. The bank of
Genoa had agreed, at excessive interest and on 40
good security, to advance the King of Spain a
sum of money sufficient to equip his vast
Armada; of which our peerless Elizabeth (more
than in name the Mother of her People) being
well informed, sent Walsingham, her wise and 45
faithful secretary, to consult the merchants of
this loyal city, who all agreed to direct their
several agents to influence, if possible, the Genoese to break their contract with the Spanish
court. 'Tis done; the state and bank of Genoa, 50
having maturely weigh'd and rightly judged of
their true interest, prefer the friendship of the
merchants of London to that of a monarch who
proudly stiles himself King of both Indies.

True. Happy success of prudent councils! 55
What an expence of blood and treasure is here
saved! Excellent Queen! O how unlike to
former princes, who made the danger of foreign
enemies a pretence to oppress their subjects by
taxes great and grievous to be borne. 60

Thor. Not so our gracious Queen, whose

43 *Armada.* 1810 corrects to Armado.
57–58 *unlike to former princes.* O4, O7, unlike those princes.
58 *who made.* O4, O7, who make.

richest exchequer is her people's love, as their
happiness her greatest glory.

True. On these terms to defend us, is to
make our protection a benefit worthy her who   65
confers it, and well worth our acceptance.—
Sir, have you any commands for me at this
time.

Thor. Only to look carefully over the files to
see whether there are any trades-mens bills un-   70
paid ; and if there are, to send and discharge 'em.
We must not let artificers lose their time, so
useful to the publick and their families, in unnecessary attendance.   [*Exit Trueman.*]

SCENE II.

[*Enter Maria.*]

Thorowgood and Maria.

Thorowgood. Well, Maria, have you given
orders for the entertainment ? I would have it
in some measure worthy the guests. Let there
be plenty, and of the best ; that the courtiers,
tho' they should deny us citizens politeness, may   5
at least commend our hospitality.

Maria. Sir, I have endeavoured not to wrong

66 *acceptance.* O1 inserts *Tr.* making the next sentence a separate speech. Correct in O4.
71 *to send.* O4, O7, send.

your well-known generosity by an ill-tim'd
parsimony.

Thor. Nay, 'twas a needless caution; I have 10
no cause to doubt your prudence.

Ma. Sir, I find myself unfit for conversation
at present; I should but increase the number of
the company without adding to their satisfac-
tion.   15

Thor. Nay, my child, this melancholy must
not be indulged.

Ma. Company will but increase it. I wish
you would dispense with my absence; solitude
best suits my present temper.   20

Thor. You are not insensible that it is chiefly
on your account these noble lords do me the
honour so frequently to grace my board; shou'd
you be absent, the disappointment may make
them repent their condescension, and think their 25
labour lost.

Ma. He that shall think his time or honour
lost in visiting you can set no real value on your
daughter's company, whose only merit is that
she is yours. The man of quality, who chuses 30
to converse with a gentleman and merchant of
your worth and character may confer honour by
so doing, but he loses none.

13 *at present.* O4, O7, omit *at present*, with (;) after *conversation*; 1810 puts a period after *at present*.

Thor. Come, come, Maria; I need not tell
you that a young gentleman may prefer your 35
conversation to mine, yet intend me no disre-
spect at all; for, tho' he may lose no honour
in my company, 'tis very natural for him to expect more pleasure in yours. I remember the
time when the company of the greatest and 40
wisest man in the kingdom would have been in-
sipid and tiresome to me, if it had deprived me
of an opportunity of enjoying your mother's.

Ma. Your's no doubt was as agreeable to
her; for generous minds know no pleasure in 45
society but where 'tis mutual.

Thor. Thou know'st I have no heir, no child
but thee; the fruits of many years successful
industry must all be thine. Now, it would give
me pleasure great as my love, to see on whom 50
you would bestow it. I am daily solicited by men
of the greatest rank and merit for leave to address
you; but I have hitherto declin'd it, in hopes
that by observation I shou'd learn which way
your inclination tends; for, as I know love to 55
be essential to happiness in the marriage state,
I had rather my approbation should confirm your
choice than direct it.

Ma. What can I say? How shall I answer, as
I ought, this tenderness, so uncommon even in the 60
best of parents? But you are without example;

yet had you been less indulgent, I had been most
wretched. That I look on the croud of courtiers
that visit here with equal esteem, but equal indifference, you have observed, and I must needs con-   65
fess; yet had you asserted your authority, and
insisted on a parent's right to be obey'd, I had
submitted, and to my duty sacrificed my peace.

Thor. From your perfect obedience in every
other instance, I fear'd as much; and therefore   70
wou'd leave you without a byass in an affair
wherein your happiness is so immediately concern'd.

Ma. Whether from a want of that just ambition that wou'd become your daughter, or from   75
some other cause, I know not; but I find high
birth and titles don't recommend the man who
owns them to my affections.

Thor. I wou'd not that they shou'd, unless
his merit recommends him more. A noble birth   80
and fortune, tho' they make not a bad man good,
yet they are a real advantage to a worthy one,
and place his virtues in the fairest light.

Ma. I cannot answer for my inclinations,
but they shall ever be submitted to your wisdom   85
and authority; and, as you will not compel me
to marry where I cannot love, so love shall never
make me act contrary to my duty. Sir, have I
your permission to retire?

Thor. I'll see you to your chamber. [*Exeunt.*]   90

SCENE III.

A Room in Millwood's House.

Millwood [at her toilet]. Lucy, waiting.

Millwood. How do I look to day, Lucy?

Lucy. O, killingly, madam! A little more red, and you'll be irresistible! But why this more than ordinary care of your dress and complexion? What new conquest are you aiming at?

Mill. A conquest wou'd be new indeed!

Lucy. Not to you, who make 'em every day, but to me.—Well! 'tis what I'm never to expect, unfortunate as I am. But your wit and beauty—

Mill. First made me a wretch, and still continue me so. Men, however generous or sincere to one another, are all selfish hypocrites in their affairs with us. We are no otherwise esteemed or regarded by them, but as we contribute to their satisfaction.

Lucy. You are certainly, madam, on the wrong side in this argument. Is not the expence all theirs? And I am sure it is our own fault, if we hav'n't our share of the pleasure.

Mill. We are but slaves to men.

Lucy. Nay, 'tis they that are slaves most certainly; for we lay them under contribution.

at her toilet, O4, O7. 1810 as O1.

Mill. Slaves have no property; no, not even 25
in themselves. All is the victor's.

Lucy. You are strangely arbitrary in your principles, madam.

Mill. I would have my conquests compleat,
like those of the Spaniards in the New World: 30
who first plunder'd the natives of all the wealth
they had, and then condemn'd the wretches to
the mines for life to work for more.

Lucy. Well, I shall never approve of your
scheme of government; I should think it much 35
more politick, as well as just, to find my subjects an easier imployment.

Mill. It's a general maxim among the knowing part of mankind, that a woman without
virtue, like a man without honour or honesty, 40
is capable of any action, tho' never so vile; and
yet, what pains will they not take, what arts
not use, to seduce us from our innocence, and
make us contemptible and wicked, even in their
own opinions! Then is it not just, the villains, 45
to their cost, should find us so.—But guilt
makes them suspicious, and keeps them on their
guard; therefore we can take advantage only of
the young and innocent part of the sex, who,
having never injured women, apprehend no 50
injury from them.

Lucy. Ay, they must be young indeed.

Mill. Such a one, I think, I have found.—
As I've passed thro' the City, I have often observ'd him receiving and paying considerable 55
sums of money; from thence I conclude he is
employed in affairs of consequence.

Lucy. Is he handsome?

Mill. Ay, ay, the stripling is well made.

Lucy. About—   60

Mill. Eighteen.

Lucy. Innocent, handsome, and about eighteen.—You'll be vastly happy.—Why, if you
manage well, you may keep him to your self
these two or three years.   65

Mill. If I manage well, I shall have done
with him much sooner. Having long had a
design on him; and, meeting him yesterday, I
made a full stop, and gazing wishfully on his
face, ask'd him his name; he blush'd, and bow- 70
ing very low, answer'd: 'George Barnwell.' I
beg'd his pardon for the freedom I had taken,
and told him that he was the person I had long
wish'd to see, and to whom I had an affair of
importance to communicate at a proper time   75
and place. He named a tavern; I talk'd of
honour and reputation, and invited him to my
house: he swallow'd the bait, promis'd to come,

59 *well made*. O4, O7, well made, and has a good face.
67 *sooner. Having*, 1810. O1 interpunctuates : sooner, having.

and this is the time I expect him. (*Knocking at the door.*) Some body knocks—d'ye hear; I am at home to no body to day but him.

[*Exit Lucy.*]

Scene IV.

Millwood.

Millwood. Less affairs must give way to those of more consequence; and I am strangely mistaken if this does not prove of great importance to me and him too, before I have done with him.—Now, after what manner shall I receive him? Let me consider—what manner of person am I to receive? He is young, innocent, and bashful; therefore I must take care not to shock him at first.—But then, if I have any skill in phisiognomy, he is amorous, and, with a little assistance, will soon get the better of his modesty.—I'll trust to nature, who does wonders in these matters.—If to seem what one is not, in order to be the better liked for what one really is; if to speak one thing, and mean the direct contrary, be art in a woman,—I know nothing of nature.

8–9 *care not to shock him.* O4, O7, care not to put him out of countenance.

12 *I'll trust.* O4, O7, I'll e'en trust.

SCENE V.

[*Millwood.*] *To her Barnwell, bowing very low.*
Lucy at a distance.

Millwood. Sir! the surprize and joy——
Barnwell. Madam——
Mill. (*advancing*). This is such a favour——
Barn. (*still advances*). Pardon me, madam——
Mill. So unhop'd for——(*Barnwell salutes her,*   5
and retires in confusion.)   To see you here.——Ex-
cuse the confusion——
Barn. I fear I am too bold.
Mill. Alas, sir! All my apprehensions pro-
ceed from my fears of your thinking me so.——   10
Please, sir, to sit.——I am as much at a loss how
to receive this honour as I ought, as I am sur-
priz'd at your goodness in confering it.
Barn. I thought you had expected me——I
promis'd to come.   15
Mill. That is the more surprizing; few men
are such religious observers of their word.
Barn. All who are honest are.
Mill. To one another.——But we silly women
are seldom thought of consequence enough to   20
gain a place in your remembrance.
                    Laying her hand on his, as by accident.

9–10 *All my . . . so.* Also 1810. O4, O7, I may justly
apprehend you think me so.
19 *silly.* Also 1810. O4, O7, 1775, simple.

Barn. (*aside*). Her disorder is so great, she don't perceive she has laid her hand on mine.—Heaven! how she trembles!—What can this mean? 25

Mill. The interest I have in all that relates to you, (the reason of which you shall know hereafter) excites my curiosity; and, were I sure you would pardon my presumption, I should desire to know your real sentiments on a very 30 particular affair.

Barn. Madam, you may command my poor thoughts on any subject; I have none that I would conceal.

Mill. You'll think me bold. 35

Barn. No, indeed.

Mill. What then are your thoughts of love?

Barn. If you mean the love of women, I have not thought of it all.—My youth and circumstances make such thoughts improper in me yet. 40 But if you mean the general love we owe to mankind, I think no one has more of it in his temper than my self.—I don't know that person in the world whose happiness I don't wish, and wou'dn't promote, were it in my power.— 45 In an especial manner I love my Uncle, and my Master, but, above all, my friend.

24 *Heaven!* O7, Heavens!
31 *affair.* O4, O7, subject.

Mill. You have a friend then whom you love?

Barn. As he does me, sincerely.   50

Mill. He is, no doubt, often bless'd with your company and conversation?

Barn. We live in one house together, and both serve the same worthy merchant.

Mill. Happy, happy youth!—Who e'er thou   55
art, I envy thee, and so must all, who see and know this youth.—What have I lost, by being form'd a woman! I hate my sex, my self. Had I been a man, I might, perhaps, have been as happy in your friendship, as he who now enjoys   60
it; but, as it is—Oh!

Barn. (*aside*). I never observ'd women before, or this is sure the most beautiful of her sex! You seem disorder'd, madam! May I know the cause?   65

Mill. Do not ask me,—I can never speak it, whatever is the cause.—I wish for things impossible.—I wou'd be a servant, bound to the same master as you are, to live in one house with you.   70

Barn. (*aside*). How strange, and yet how kind, her words and actions are? And the effect they have on me is as strange. I feel desires I never

---

57 *know this youth.* 1810 absurdly inserts [*Aside*].
69 *as you are.* O4, O7, omit.

knew before;—I must be gone, while I have power to go. Madam, I humbly take my leave. 75

Mill. You will not sure leave me so soon!

Barn. Indeed I must.

Mill. You cannot be so cruel!—I have prepar'd a poor supper, at which I promis'd my self your company. 80

Barn. I am sorry I must refuse the honour that you design'd me—but my duty to my master calls me hence. I never yet neglected his service; he is so gentle, and so good a master, that, should I wrong him, tho' he might forgive 85 me, I never should forgive my self.

Mill. Am I refus'd, by the first man, the second favour I ever stoop'd to ask?—Go then, thou proud hard-hearted youth!—But know, you are the only man that cou'd be found, who 90 would let me sue twice for greater favours.

Barn. What shall I do!—How shall I go or stay!

Mill. Yet do not, do not, leave me! I wish my sex's pride wou'd meet your scorn:—But 95 when I look upon you,—when I behold those eyes,—Oh! spare my tongue, and let my blushes speak.—This flood of tears to that will force

94 *I wish.* O4, O7, I with.

97–99 *blushes speak . . . their way, and declare.* O4, blushes (this flood of tears to that will force its way) declare. O7 has the same as O4 except for a (—) after *blushes.*

their way, and declare—what woman's modesty
should hide.   100

Barn. Oh, heavens! she loves me, worthless
as I am; her looks, her words, her flowing tears
confess it;—and can I leave her then?—Oh,
never, never!—Madam, dry up those tears!
You shall command me always; I will stay here 105
for ever, if you'd have me.

Lucy (aside). So! she has wheedled him out
of his virtue of obedience already, and will strip
him of all the rest, one after another, 'till she
has left him as few as her ladyship, or my self. 110

Mill. Now you are kind, indeed; but I mean
not to detain you always. I would have you
shake off all slavish obedience to your master;
but you may serve him still.

Lucy (aside). Serve him still!—Aye, or he'll 115
have no opportunity of fingering his cash, and
then he'll not serve your end, I'll be sworn.

Scene VI.

To them Blunt.

Blunt. Madam, supper's on the table.

Mill. Come, sir, you'll excuse all defects.—
My thoughts were too much employ'd on my
guest to observe the entertainment.

[*Exeunt Millwood and Barnwell.*]

104 *those.* O4, O7, your.

Scene VII.

Lucy and Blunt.

Blunt. What ! is all this preparation, this elegant supper, variety of wines, and musick, for the entertainment of that young fellow ?

Lucy. So it seems.

Blunt. What ! is our mistress turn'd fool at 5
last ? She's in love with him, I suppose.

Lucy. I suppose not ; but she designs to make him in love with her, if she can.

Blunt. What will she get by that ? He seems under age, and can't be suppos'd to have much 10
money.

Lucy. But his master has ; and that's the same thing, as she'll manage it.

Blunt. I don't like this fooling with a handsome young fellow ; while she's endeavouring to 15
ensnare him, she may be caught her self.

Lucy. Nay, were she like me, that would certainly be the consequence ; for, I confess, there is something in youth and innocence that moves me mightily. 20

Blunt. Yes, so does the smoothness and plumpness of a partridge move a mighty desire in the hawk to be the destruction of it.

Lucy. Why, birds are their prey, as men are

5 *What ! is.* O4, O7, What's.

ours; though, as you observ'd, we are some- 25
times caught our selves; but that I dare say will
never be the case with our mistress.

Blunt. I wish it may prove so; for you know
we all depend upon her. Should she trifle away
her time with a young fellow, that there's no- 30
thing to be got by, we must all starve.

Lucy. There's no danger of that, for I am sure
she has no view in this affair but interest.

Blunt. Well, and what hopes are there of
success in that? 35

Lucy. The most promising that can be. 'Tis
true, the youth has his scruples; but she'll soon
teach him to answer them, by stifling his conscience. O, the lad is in a hopeful way, depend
upon't.   [*Exeunt.*] 40

Scene VIII.

Barnwell and Millwood at an entertainment.

Barnwell. What can I answer? All that I
know is, that you are fair, and I am miserable.

Millwood. We are both so, and yet the fault
is in ourselves.

Barn. To ease our present anguish, by plung- 5

Scene VIII. O4, O7, have: Scene draws and discovers Barnwell and Millwood at supper. An entertainment of music and
singing. After which they come forward. 1810: Barnwell and
Millwood with an entertainment and singing.

ing into guilt, is to buy a moment's pleasure with an age of pain.

Mill. I should have thought the joys of love as lasting as they are great. If ours prove otherwise, 'tis your inconstancy must make them so. 10

Barn. The law of Heaven will not be revers'd; and that requires us to govern our passions.

Mill. To give us sense of beauty and desires, and yet forbid us to taste and be happy, is cruelty to nature.—Have we passions only to torment us? 15

Barn. To hear you talk, tho' in the cause of vice—to gaze upon your beauty—press your hand—and see your snow-white bosom heave 20 and fall—enflames my wishes. My pulse beats high—my senses all are in a hurry, and I am on the rack of wild desire. Yet, for a moment's guilty pleasure, shall I lose my innocence, my peace of mind, and hopes of solid happiness? 25

Mill. Chimeras all!—Come on with me and prove:
No joy's like woman kind, nor Heav'n like love.

Barn. I wou'd not, yet must on.—

26 *Chimeras all, &c.,* O7. O1, O4, drop *Come on . . . love* below *chimeras all,* which they print in roman.

28 *yet must on,* O4, O7. O1 and 1810, yet I must on.

Reluctant thus, the merchant quits his ease,
And trusts to rocks, and sands, and stormy seas ;   30
In hopes some unknown golden coast to find,
Commits himself, tho' doubtful, to the wind ;
Longs much for joys to come, yet mourns those left
*   behind.*

The End of the First Act.

Act II.

Scene I. *A Room in Thorowgood's House.*

[*Enter*] *Barnwell.*

Barnwell. How strange are all things round me! Like some thief, who treads forbidden ground, fearful I enter each apartment of this well known house. To guilty love, as if that was too little, already have I added breach of 5
trust.—A thief!—Can I know my self that wretched thing, and look my honest friend and injured master in the face? Tho' hypocrisy may a while conceal my guilt, at length it will be known, and publick shame and ruin must ensue. 10
In the mean time, what must be my life? Ever to speak a language foreign to my heart; hourly to add to the number of my crimes in order to conceal 'em.—Sure, such was the condition of the grand apostate, when first he lost his purity; 15
like me, disconsolate he wander'd, and, while yet in Heaven, bore all his future Hell about him.

[*Enter Trueman.*]

3 *ground.* O4, O7, 1775, add after this word: and fain wou'd lurk unseen. This is again omitted in 1810.
5 *was.* O4, O7, were.

Scene II.

Barnwell and Trueman.

Trueman. Barnwell! O how I rejoice to see you safe! So will our master and his gentle daughter, who during your absence often inquir'd after you.

Barnwell (aside). Wou'd he were gone! His 5 officious love will pry into the secrets of my soul.

True. Unless you knew the pain the whole family has felt on your account, you can't conceive how much you are belov'd. But why thus cold and silent? When my heart is full of joy 10 for your return, why do you turn away? why thus avoid me? What have I done? how am I alter'd since you saw me last? Or rather, what have you done? and why are you thus changed, for I am still the same. 15

Barn. (aside). What have I done, indeed?

True. Not speak nor look upon me!

Barn. (aside). By my face he will discover all I wou'd conceal; methinks, already I begin to hate him. 20

True. I cannot bear this usage from a friend —one whom till now I ever found so loving, whom yet I love, tho' this unkindness strikes at the root of friendship, and might destroy it in any breast but mine. 25

Barn. (*turning to him*). I am not well. Sleep has been a stranger to these eyes since you beheld them last.

True. Heavy they look indeed, and swoln with tears ;—now they o'erflow. Rightly did my sympathizing heart forbode last night, when thou wast absent, something fatal to our peace.

Barn. Your friendship ingages you too far. My troubles, whate'er they are, are mine alone ; you have no interest in them, nor ought your concern for me give you a moment's pain.

True. You speak as if you knew of friendship nothing but the name. Before I saw your grief I felt it. Since we parted last I have slept no more than you, but pensive in my chamber sat alone, and spent the tedious night in wishes for your safety and return ; e'en now, tho' ignorant of the cause, your sorrow wounds me to the heart.

Barn. 'Twill not be always thus. Friendship and all engagements cease, as circumstances and occasions vary ; and, since you once may hate me, perhaps it might be better for us both that now you lov'd me less.

True. Sure, I but dream ! Without a cause would Barnwell use me thus ? Ungenerous and ungrateful youth, farewell !—I shall endeavour to follow your advice. (*Going.*) [*Aside.*] Yet

stay, perhaps I am too rash, and angry when
the cause demands compassion. Some unfore- 55
seen calamity may have befaln him, too great to
bear.

Barn. [*aside*]. What part am I reduc'd to
act ! 'Tis vile and base to move his temper
thus—the best of friends and men ! 60

True. I am to blame ; prithee forgive me,
Barnwell !—Try to compose your ruffled mind ;
and let me know the cause that thus transports
you from your self : my friendly counsel may
restore your peace. 65

Barn. All that is possible for man to do for
man, your generous friendship may effect ; but
here even that's in vain.

True. Something dreadful is labouring in
your breast. O give it vent, and let me share 70
your grief ; 'twill ease your pain, shou'd it
admit no cure, and make it lighter by the part
I bear.

Barn. Vain supposition ! My woes increase
by being observ'd ; shou'd the cause be known, 75
they wou'd exceed all bounds.

True. So well I know thy honest heart, guilt
cannot harbour there.

Barn. (*aside*). O torture insupportable !

True. Then why am I excluded ? Have I a 80
thought I would conceal from you.

Barn. If still you urge me on this hated subject, I'll never enter more beneath this roof, nor see your face again.

True. 'Tis strange—but I have done. Say 85 but you hate me not!

Barn. Hate you! I am not that monster yet.

True. Shall our friendship still continue?

Barn. It's a blessing I never was worthy of; 90 yet now must stand on terms, and but upon conditions can confirm it.

True. What are they?

Barn. Never hereafter, tho' you shou'd wonder at my conduct, desire to know more than 95 I am willing to reveal.

True. 'Tis hard; but upon any conditions I must be your friend.

Barn. Then, as much as one lost to himself can be another's, I am yours. *Embracing.* 100

True. Be ever so, and may Heav'n restore your peace!

Barn. Will yesterday return? We have heard the glorious sun, that till then incessant roll'd, once stopp'd his rapid course, and once 105 went back. The dead have risen, and parched rocks pour'd forth a liquid stream to quench a peoples thirst; the sea divided, and form'd walls of water, while a whole nation pass'd in safety

thro' its sandy bosom; hungry lions have re-110
fus'd their prey, and men unhurt have walk'd
amidst consuming flames. But never yet did
time, once past, return.

True. Tho' the continued chain of time has
never once been broke, nor ever will, but unin-115
terrupted must keep on its course, till lost in
eternity it ends there where it first begun : yet,
as Heav'n can repair whatever evils time can
bring upon us, he who trusts Heav'n ought never
to despair. But business requires our attend-120
ance—business, the youth's best preservative
from ill, as idleness his worst of snares. Will
you go with me ?

Barn. I'll take a little time to reflect on what
has past, and follow you. [*Exit Trueman.*] 125

SCENE III.

Barnwell.

Barnwell. I might have trusted Trueman to
have applied to my uncle to have repaired the
wrong I have done my master,—but what of
Millwood ? Must I expose her too ? Ungener-

119–120 *us, he who . . . despair.* O4, O7, us, we ought
never to despair.

1–2 *Trueman to have applied to my uncle to have repaired,* O1
and 1810. Q4, O7, Trueman, and ingaged him to apply to my
uncle to repair.

ous and base! Then Heav'n requires it not.— 5
But Heaven requires that I forsake her. What!
never see her more! Does Heaven require that?
—I hope I may see her, and Heav'n not be
offended. Presumptuous hope—dearly already
have I prov'd my frailty; should I once more 10
tempt Heav'n, I may be left to fall never to rise
again. Yet shall I leave her, for ever leave her,
and not let her know the cause? She who loves
me with such a boundless passion—can cruelty
be duty? I judge of what she then must feel by 15
what I now indure. The love of life and fear of
shame, oppos'd by inclination strong as death or
shame, like wind and tide in raging conflict met,
when neither can prevail, keep me in doubt.
How then can I determine? 20

Scene IV.

[*Enter Thorowgood.*]

Thorowgood and Barnwell.

Thorowgood. Without a cause assign'd, or
notice given, to absent your self last night was
a fault, young man, and I came to chide you for
it, but hope I am prevented. That modest blush,
the confusion so visible in your face, speak grief 5
and shame. When we have offended Heaven,

20 *determine*, O4, O7. O1, *determines*.

it requires no more; and shall man, who needs
himself to be forgiven, be harder to appease?
If my pardon or love be of moment to your peace,
look up, secure of both.   10

Barnwell (*aside*). This goodness has o'er
come me.—O sir! you know not the nature and
extent of my offence; and I shou'd abuse your
mistaken bounty to receive 'em. Tho' I had
rather die than speak my shame; tho' racks   15
could not have forced the guilty secret from my
breast, your kindness has.

Thor. Enough, enough, whate'er it be, this
concern shows you're convinc'd, and I am satisfied. [*Aside.*] How painful is the sense of guilt 20
to an ingenuous mind—some youthful folly
which it were prudent not to enquire into.—
When we consider the frail condition of humanity, it may raise our pity, not our wonder, that
youth should go astray: when reason, weak at 25
the best when oppos'd to inclination, scarce
form'd, and wholly unassisted by experience,
faintly contends, or willingly becomes the slave
of sense. The state of youth is much to be de-
plored; and the more so, because they see it 30
not: they being then to danger most expos'd,
when they are least prepar'd for their defence.

14 *receive 'em.* O1, 1810. O4, O7, receive it.
26 *best when oppos'd.* O4, O7, best opposed.
32 *defence.* After this O7, 1775, 1810, print [*Aside.*

Barn. It will be known, and you recall your pardon and abhor me.

Thor. I never will; so Heav'n confirm to 35 me the pardon of my offences! Yet be upon your guard in this gay, thoughtless season of your life; now, when the sense of pleasure's quick, and passion high, the voluptuous appetites raging and fierce demand the strongest 40 curb, take heed of a relapse: when vice becomes habitual, the very power of leaving it is lost.

Barn. Hear me, then, on my knees confess—

Thor. I will not hear a syllable more upon this subject; it were not mercy, but cruelty, to 45 hear what must give you such torment to reveal.

Barn. This generosity amazes and distracts me.

Thor. This remorse makes thee dearer to me than if thou hadst never offended; whatever is your fault, of this I'm certain: 'twas harder for 50 you to offend than me to pardon.   [*Exit.*]

Scene V.

Barnwell.

Barnwell. Villain, villain, villain! basely to wrong so excellent a man! Shou'd I again return to folly—detested thought—but what of

35–36 *so Heav'n . . . offences.* O4, O7, omit.
38 *life; now, when.* O7, life, when.   43 *then.* O4, O7, omit.
44 *I will not hear a.* O4, O7, Not a.

Millwood then?—Why, I renounce her;—I
give her up:—the struggle's over and virtue has   5
prevail'd. Reason may convince, but gratitude
compels. This unlook'd for generosity has sav'd
me from destruction.   *Going.*

Scene VI.

[Barnwell.] To him a Footman.

Footman. Sir, two ladies from your uncle in
the country desire to see you.

Barn. (aside). Who shou'd they be? — Tell
them I'll wait upon 'em.   *[Exit Footman.]*

Scene VII.

Barnwell.

Barnwell. Methinks I dread to see 'em.
Guilt, what a coward hast thou made me!
Now every thing alarms me.

Scene VIII.

Another Room in Thorowgood's House.

Millwood and Lucy; and to them a Footman.

Footman. Ladies, he'll wait upon you immediately.

Millwood. 'Tis very well.—I thank you.
                              [Exit Footman.]

Scene VII. 2 *Guilt . . . made me!—Now . . . me.* O4, O7,
transpose the two sentences.

Scene IX.

Millwood and Lucy.

[Enter Barnwell.]

Barnwell. Confusion! Millwood!

Millwood. That angry look tells me that here I'm an unwelcome guest. I fear'd as much— the unhappy are so everywhere.

Barn. Will nothing but my utter ruin content you? 5

Mill. Unkind and cruel! Lost my self, your happiness is now my only care.

Barn. How did you gain admission?

Mill. Saying we were desir'd by your uncle to 10 visit and deliver a message to you, we were receiv'd by the family without suspicion, and with much respect directed here.

Barn. Why did you come at all?

Mill. I never shall trouble you more; I'm 15 come to take my leave for ever. Such is the malice of my fate. I go hopeless, despairing ever to return. This hour is all I have left me. One short hour is all I have to bestow on love and you, for whom I thought the longest life too 20 short.

Barn. Then we are met to part for ever?

13 *directed*, O1, 1810. O7, conducted.
18 *left me*, O1, 1810. O4, O7, omit *me*.

Mill. It must be so—yet think not that time or absence ever shall put a period to my grief or make me love you less; tho' I must 25 leave you, yet condemn me not!

Barn. Condemn you? No, I approve your resolution, and rejoice to hear it. 'Tis just; 'tis necessary; I have well weigh'd, and found it so. 30

Lucy (aside). I'm afraid the young man has more sense than she thought he had.

Barn. Before you came, I had determin'd never to see you more.

Mill. (aside). Confusion! 35

Lucy (aside). Ay! we are all out; this is a turn so unexpected, that I shall make nothing of my part; they must e'en play the scene betwixt themselves.

Mill. 'Twas some relief to think, tho' absent, 40 you would love me still. But to find, tho' fortune had been kind, that you, more cruel and inconstant, had resolv'd to cast me off—this, as I never cou'd expect, I have not learnt to bear.

Barn. I am sorry to hear you blame in me a 45 resolution that so well becomes us both.

Mill. I have reason for what I do, but you have none.

24 *ever shall.* O4, O7, shall ever.
41 *still. But.* All the editions, still ; but.
42 *kind.* O4, O7, indulgent.

Barn. Can we want a reason for parting, who have so many to wish we never had met? 50

Mill. Look on me, Barnwell! Am I deform'd or old, that satiety so soon succeeds enjoyment? Nay, look again, am I not she whom yesterday you thought the fairest and the kindest of her sex? whose hand, trembling with extacy, 55 you prest and moulded thus, while on my eyes you gazed with such delight, as if desire increas'd by being fed?

Barn. No more; let me repent my former follies, if possible, without remembring what 60 they were.

Mill. Why?

Barn. Such is my frailty that 'tis dangerous.

Mill. Where is the danger, since we are to part? 65

Barn. The thought of that already is too painful.

Mill. If it be painful to part, then I may hope at least you do not hate me?

Barn. No—no—I never said I did.—O my 70 heart!—

Mill. Perhaps you pity me?

Barn. I do—I do—indeed, I do.

Mill. You'll think upon me?

Barn. Doubt it not, while I can think at all! 75

Mill. You may judge an embrace at parting

too great a favour, though it would be the last?
(*He draws back*.) A look shall then suffice—
farewell for ever.   [*Exit with Lucy*.]

SCENE X.

Barnwell.

Barnwell. If to resolve to suffer be to conquer, I have conquer'd. Painful victory!

SCENE XI.

[*Reënter Millwood and Lucy.*]

Barnwell, Millwood and Lucy.

Millwood. One thing I had forgot: I never
must return to my own house again. This I
thought proper to let you know, lest your mind
shou'd change, and you shou'd seek in vain to
find me there. Forgive me this second intrusion;   5
I only came to give you this caution; and that
perhaps was needless.

Barnwell. I hope it was; yet it is kind, and
I must thank you for it.

Mill. (*to Lucy*). My friend, your arm.——   10
Now I am gone for ever.   *Going*.

Barn. One thing more: sure, there's no
danger in my knowing where you go?—If you
think otherwise——

Mill. (*weeping*). Alas! 15

Lucy (*aside*). We are right, I find; that's my cue. Ah; dear sir, she's going she knows not whither; but go she must.

Barn. Humanity obliges me to wish you well: why will you thus expose your self to needless 20 troubles?

Lucy. Nay, there's no help for it. She must quit the town immediately, and the kingdom as soon as possible; it was no small matter, you may be sure, that could make her resolve to 25 leave you.

Mill. No more, my friend; since he for whose dear sake alone I suffer, and am content to suffer, is kind and pities me. Wheree'er I wander through wilds and desarts, benighted and 30 forlorn, that thought shall give me comfort.

Barn. For my sake! O tell me how; which way am I so curs'd as to bring such ruin on thee?

Mill. No matter, I am contented with my 35 lot.

Barn. Leave me not in this incertainty!

Mill. I have said too much.

Barn. How, how am I the cause of your undoing? 40

18 *whither*, O4, O7. O1 only, *whether*.
29 *Wheree'er.* O4, O7, Whene'er.
30 *wilds*, O7. O1, O4, *wiles*.

Mill. 'Twill but increase your troubles.

Barn. My troubles can't be greater than they are.

Lucy. Well, well, sir; if she won't satisfy you, I will.   45

Barn. I am bound to you beyond expression.

Mill. Remember, sir, that I desir'd you not to hear it.

Barn. Begin, and ease my racking expectation!   50

Lucy. Why, you must know, my lady here was an only child; but her parents, dying while she was young, left her and her fortune (no inconsiderable one, I assure you) to the care of a gentleman who has a good estate of his own.   55

Mill. Ay, ay, the barbarous man is rich enough—but what are riches when compared to love?

Lucy. For a while he perform'd the office of a faithful guardian, settled her in a house, hir'd   60 her servants—but you have seen in what manner she liv'd, so I need say no more of that.

Mill. How I shall live hereafter, Heaven knows!

Lucy. All things went on as one cou'd wish,   65 till, some time ago, his wife dying, he fell violently in love with his charge, and wou'd fain

41 *'Twill but.* O4, O7, 1775, 1810, To know it will but.

have marry'd her. Now, the man is neither old
nor ugly, but a good personable sort of a man;
but I don't know how it was she cou'd never 70
endure him. In short, her ill usage so provok'd
him, that he brought in an account of his execu-
torship, wherein he makes her debtor to him —

Mill. A trifle in it self, but more than enough
to ruin me, whom, by this unjust account, he 75
had stripp'd of all before.

Lucy. Now, she having neither money, nor
friend, except me, who am as unfortunate as
her self, he compell'd her to pass his account,
and give bond for the sum he demanded; but 80
still provided handsomely for her, and continued
his courtship, till, being inform'd by his spies
(truly I suspect some in her own family) that
you were entertain'd at her house, and stay'd
with her all night, he came this morning raving 85
and storming like a madman; talks no more of
marriage—so there's no hopes of making up
matters that way—but vows her ruin, unless
she'll allow him the same favour that he sup-
poses she granted you. 90

Barn. Must she be ruin'd, or find her refuge
in another's arms?

Mill. He gave me but an hour to resolve in.
That's happily spent with you—and now I go.—

75 *this.* O7, his.

Barn. To be expos'd to all the rigours of the 95
various seasons, the summer's parching heat,
and winter's cold; unhous'd to wander friendless thro' the unhospitable world, in misery and
want, attended with fear and danger, and pursu'd by malice and revenge—woud'st thou en- 100
dure all this for me, and can I do nothing,
nothing to prevent it?

Lucy. 'Tis really a pity there can be no way
found out!

Barn. O where are all my resolutions now? 105
Like early vapours, or the morning dew, chas'd
by the sun's warm beams, they're vanish'd and
lost, as tho' they had never been.

Lucy. Now, I advis'd her, sir, to comply with
the gentleman; that wou'd not only put an end 110
to her troubles, but make her fortune at once.

Barn. Tormenting fiend, away!—I had
rather perish, nay, see her perish, than have her
sav'd by him; I will my self prevent her ruin,
tho' with my own.—A moment's patience; I'll 115
return immediately.   [*Exit.*]

Scene XII.

Millwood and Lucy.

Lucy. 'Twas well you came; or, by what I
can perceive, you had lost him.

98 *world.* Earlier texts: world, in misery and want; attended.

Millwood. That, I must confess, was a danger I did not foresee; I was only afraid he should have come without money. You know 5 a house of entertainment like mine is not kept with nothing.

Lucy. That's very true; but then you shou'd be reasonable in your demands; 'tis pity to discourage a young man. 10

Scene XIII.

[Enter] Barnwell [with a bag of money].
Millwood and Lucy.

Barnwell [aside]. What am I about to do!—
Now you, who boast your reason all-sufficient, suppose your selves in my condition, and determine for me : whether it's right to let her suffer for my faults, or, by this small addition to my 5 guilt, prevent the ill effects of what is past.

Lucy. These young sinners think every thing in the ways of wickedness so strange; but I cou'd tell him that this is nothing but what's very common; for one vice as naturally begets 10 another, as a father a son. But he'll find out that himself, if he lives long enough.

Sc. *XII.* 7 *with nothing,* O1. O4, O7, *without expence.*
Sc. *XII.* 10 *discourage a young man.* O4, O7, add : *Mill.* Leave that to me. *with a bag of money,* O4, O7.
Sc. *XIII.* 11–12 *But . . . enough.* O7 prints after this *[Aside.*

Barn. Here, take this, and with it purchase
your deliverance ; return to your house, and live
in peace and safety.   15

Mill. So I may hope to see you there again.

Barn. Answer me not, but fly—lest, in the
agonies of my remorse, I take again what is not
mine to give, and abandon thee to want and
misery !   20

Mill. Say but you'll come !

Barn. You are my fate, my heaven, or my
hell ; only leave me now, dispose of me hereafter
as you please.   [*Exeunt Millwood and Lucy.*]

Scene XIV.

Barnwell.

Barnwell. What have I done !—Were my resolutions founded on reason, and sincerely made
—why then has Heaven suffer'd me to fall ? I
sought not the occasion ; and, if my heart de-
ceives me not, compassion and generosity were   5
my motives.—Is virtue inconsistent with it self,
or are vice and virtue only empty names ? Or
do they depend on accidents, beyond our power
to produce or to prevent—wherein we have no
part, and yet must be determin'd by the event ?   10
But why should I attempt to reason ? All is

17 *lest*, O4, O7. O1 only, least.

confusion, horror, and remorse : I find I am lost,
cast down from all my late erected hopes, and
plung'd again in guilt, yet scarce know how or
why—   15

 Such undistinguish'd horrors make my brain,
 Like Hell, the seat of darkness and of pain.

The End of the Second Act.

Act III.

Scene I. [*A Room in Thorowgood's House.*]

Thorowgood and Trueman [*sitting at a table with account books*].

Thorowgood. Methinks, I wou'd not have you only learn the method of merchandize, and practise it hereafter, merely as a means of getting wealth. 'Twill be well worth your pains to study it as a science. See how it is founded in reason, and the nature of things; how it has promoted humanity, as it has opened and yet keeps up an intercourse between nations, far remote from one another in situation, customs and religion; promoting arts, industry, peace and plenty; by mutual benefits diffusing mutual love from pole to pole. 5 10

Trueman. Something of this I have consider'd, and hope, by your assistance, to extend my thoughts much farther. I have observ'd those countries, where trade is promoted and encouraged, do not make discoveries to destroy, but to 15

Sitting at a table with account books, 1810.

5 *science. See.* O4, O7, science, to see.

6–7 *how it has promoted.* O4, O7, how it promotes. 1810, period after *things.*

improve, mankind by love and friendship; to tame
the fierce and polish the most savage; to teach
them the advantages of honest traffick, by taking 20
from them, with their own consent, their useless
superfluities, and giving them, in return, what,
from their ignorance in manual arts, their situation, or some other accident, they stand in need
of.   25

Thor. 'Tis justly observ'd : the populous East,
luxuriant, abounds with glittering gems, bright
pearls, aromatick spices, and health-restoring
drugs. The late found Western World glows
with unnumber'd veins of gold and silver ore. 30
On every climate and on every country, Heaven
has bestowed some good peculiar to it self.
It is the industrious merchant's business to col-
lect the various blessings of each soil and climate,
and, with the product of the whole, to enrich his 35
native country.—Well! I have examin'd your
accounts : they are not only just, as I have always found them, but regularly kept, and fairly
enter'd. I commend your diligence. Method in
business is the surest guide. He who neglects 40
it frequently stumbles, and always wanders per-
plex'd, uncertain, and in danger.—Are Barnwell's

18 *improve, mankind . . . to tame,* 1810. O1 punctuates :
improve mankind, — by love and friendship to tame. O4, O7,
place (;) after *mankind.*   23 *manual arts.* O7, mutual arts.
  29 *World glows.* O4, O7, World's rich earth glows.

accounts ready for my inspection? He does not
use to be the last on these occasions.

True. Upon receiving your orders he retir'd, 45
I thought, in some confusion. If you please,
I'll go and hasten him.——I hope he hasn't been
guilty of any neglect.

Thor. I'm now going to the Exchange; let
him know, at my return, I expect to find him 50
ready.   [*Exeunt.*]

Scene II.

[Enter] Maria with a book; sits and reads.

Maria. How forcible is truth! The weakest
mind, inspir'd with love of that, fix'd and collected in it self, with indifference beholds——the
united force of earth and Hell opposing. Such
souls are rais'd above the sense of pain, or so   5
supported that they regard it not. The martyr
cheaply purchases his heaven. Small are his sufferings, great is his reward; not so the wretch,
who combats love with duty; when the mind,
weaken'd and dissolved by the soft passion,   10
feeble and hopeless opposes its own desires.——
What is an hour, a day, a year of pain, to a
whole life of tortures, such as these?

Scene III.

[Enter Trueman.]

Trueman and Maria.

Trueman. O, Barnwell! O, my Friend, how art thou fallen!

Maria. Ha! Barnwell! What of him? Speak, say, what of Barnwell?

True. 'Tis not to be conceal'd. I've news 5 to tell of him that will afflict your generous father, your self, and all who knew him.

Ma. Defend us Heaven!

True. I cannot speak it.—See there.

Gives a letter. Maria reads.

Trueman, 10

I know my absence will surprize my honour'd master and your self; and the more, when you shall understand that the reason of my withdrawing, is my having embezzled part of the cash with which I was entrusted. After this, 'tis needless to inform 15 you that I intend never to return again. Though this might have been known by examining my accounts, yet, to prevent that unnecessary trouble, and to cut off all fruitless expectations of my return, I have left this from the lost 20

George Barnwell.

7 *knew him.* O7, know him.

Doesn't Know what virtue is

True. Lost indeed! Yet, how he shou'd be guilty of what he there charges himself withal, raises my wonder equal to my grief. Never had youth a higher sense of virtue: justly he 25 thought, and as he thought he practised; never was life more regular than his; an understanding uncommon at his years—an open, generous, manliness of temper—his manners easy, unaffected and engaging. 30

Ma. This and much more you might have said with truth. He was the delight of every eye, and joy of every heart that knew him.

True. Since such he was, and was my friend, can I support his loss?—See! the fairest and 35 happiest maid this wealthy city boasts, kindly condescends to weep for thy unhappy fate, poor ruin'd Barnwell!

Ma. Trueman, do you think a soul so delicate as his, so sensible of shame, can e'er sub- 40 mit to live a slave to vice?

True. Never, never! So well I know him, I'm sure this act of his, so contrary to his nature, must have been caused by some unavoidable necessity. 45

Ma. Is there no means yet to preserve him?

True. O, that there were! But few men recover reputation lost—a merchant never. Nor wou'd he, I fear, though I shou'd find him,

ever be brought to look his injur'd master in the 50
face.

Ma. I fear as much—and therefore wou'd
never have my father know it.

True. That's impossible.

Ma. What's the sum? 55

True. 'Tis considerable. I've mark'd it here,
to show it, with the letter, to your father, at his
return.

Ma. If I shou'd supply the money, cou'd you
so dispose of that, and the account, as to conceal 60
this unhappy mismanagement from my father?

True. Nothing more easy. But can you intend it? Will you save a helpless wretch from
ruin? Oh! 'twere an act worthy such exalted
virtue as Maria's. Sure, Heaven, in mercy to 65
my friend, inspired the generous thought!

Ma. Doubt not but I wou'd purchase so great
a happiness at a much dearer price.—But how
shall he be found?

True. Trust to my diligence for that. In 70
the mean time, I'll conceal his absence from
your father, or find such excuses for it, that the
real cause shall never be suspected.

Ma. In attempting to save from shame one
whom we hope may yet return to virtue, to 75
Heaven, and you, the judges of this action, I

76 *the judges,* O1. O4, O7, the only witnesses.

appeal, whether I have done any thing misbe-
coming my sex and character.

True. Earth must approve the deed, and
Heaven, I doubt not, will reward it.   80

Ma. If Heaven succeed it, I am well rewarded. A virgin's fame is sullied by suspicion's
slightest breath; and therefore as this must be
a secret from my father and the world, for Barnwell's sake, for mine, let it be so to him!   85

[*Exeunt.*]

Scene IV.

Millwood's House. [*Enter*] *Lucy and Blunt.*

Lucy. Well! what do you think of Millwood's conduct now!

Blunt. I own it is surprizing; I don't know
which to admire most, her feign'd or his real
passion—tho' I have sometimes been afraid that   5
her avarice wou'd discover her. But his youth
and want of experience make it the easier to
impose on him.

Lucy. No, it is his love. To do him justice,
notwithstanding his youth, he don't want under-   10
standing; but you men are much easier imposed
on, in these affairs, than your vanity will allow
you to believe. Let me see the wisest of you all
as much in love with me as Barnwell is with

77 *have done.* O4, O7, do.   81 *succeed.* O4, O7, succeeds.

Millwood, and I'll engage to make as great a 15
fool of him.

Blunt. And all circumstances consider'd, to
make as much money of him too.

Lucy. I can't answer for that. Her artifice
in making him rob his master at first, and the 20
various stratagems by which she has obliged him
to continue in that course, astonish even me, who
know her so well.

Blunt. But then you are to consider that the
money was his master's. 25

Lucy. There was the difficulty of it. Had it
been his own it had been nothing. Were the
world his, she might have it for a smile.—But
those golden days are done; he's ruin'd, and
Millwood's hopes of farther profits there, are at 30
an end.

Blunt. That's no more than we all expected.

Lucy. Being call'd by his master to make up
his accounts, he was forc'd to quit his house and
service, and wisely flies to Millwood for relief 35
and entertainment.

Blunt. I have not heard of this before! How
did she receive him?

Lucy. As you wou'd expect. She wonder'd
what he meant; was astonish'd at his impu- 40
dence; and, with an air of modesty peculiar to

22 *continue in.* O4, O7, continue.

her self, swore so heartily that she never saw
him before, that she put me out of countenance.

Blunt. That's much indeed! But how did
Barnwell behave?

Lucy. He griev'd, and, at length, enrag'd at
this barbarous treatment, was preparing to be
gone; and, making toward the door, show'd
a bag of money, which he had stol'n from his
master—the last he's ever like to have from
thence.

Blunt. But then, Millwood?

Lucy. Aye, she, with her usual address, return'd to her old arts of lying, swearing and dis-
sembling. Hung on his neck, and wept, and
swore 'twas meant in jest; till the easy fool,
melted into tears, threw the money into her
lap, and swore he had rather die than think her
false.

Blunt. Strange infatuation!

Lucy. But what follow'd was stranger still.
As doubts and fears, follow'd by reconcilement,
ever increase love, where the passion is sincere:
so in him it caus'd so wild a transport of excess-

---

48 *and, making.* O4, O7, when, making.
  show'd, O1. O4, O7, he show'd.
49 *a bag.* O4, O7, a sum. *stol'n.* O4, O7, brought.
50 *master.* O4, O7, master's.
55 *and wept.* O7, wept.
56 *the easy fool,* O1. O4, O7, the amorous youth.

ive fondness, such joy, such grief, such pleas- 65
ure, and such anguish, that nature in him seem'd
sinking with the weight, and the charm'd soul
dispos'd to quit his breast for hers. Just then,
when every passion with lawless anarchy prevail'd, and reason was in the raging tempest lost, 70
the cruel, artful Millwood prevail'd upon the
wretched youth to promise what I tremble but
to think on.

Blunt. I am amaz'd! What can it be?

Lucy. You will be more so, to hear it is to 75
attempt the life of his nearest relation, and best
benefactor.

Blunt. His uncle, whom we have often heard
him speak of as a gentleman of a large estate
and fair character in the country, where he lives? 80

Lucy. The same. She was no sooner possess'd of the last dear purchase of his ruin, but
her avarice, insatiate as the grave, demands this
horrid sacrifice—Barnwell's near relation; and
unsuspected virtue must give too easy means to 85
seize the good man's treasure, whose blood must
seal the dreadful secret, and prevent the terrors
of her guilty fears.

Blunt. Is it possible she cou'd perswade him
to do an act like that? He is, by nature, hon- 90
est, grateful, compassionate, and generous; and

83 *demands.* O4, O7, demanded.

though his love and her artful perswasions have
wrought him to practise what he most abhors;
yet we all can witness for him with what reluctance he has still comply'd! So many tears 95
he shed o'er each offence, as might, if possible,
sanctify theft, and make a merit of a crime.

Lucy. 'Tis true; at the naming the murder
of his uncle he started into rage, and, breaking
from her arms, where she till then had held 100
him with well dissembled love and false en-
dearments, call'd her "cruel monster, devil," and
told her she was born for his destruction. She
thought it not for her purpose to meet his rage
with rage, but affected a most passionate fit of 105
grief — rail'd at her fate, and curs'd her way-
ward stars : that still her wants shou'd force her
to press him to act such deeds as she must needs
abhor, as well as he; but told him, necessity had
no law, and love no bounds; that therefore he 110
never truly lov'd, but meant, in her necessity,
to forsake her; then kneel'd and swore, that
since, by his refusal, he had given her cause to
doubt his love, she never wou'd see him more
—unless, to prove it true, he robb'd his uncle to 115
supply her wants, and murder'd him, to keep it
from discovery.

Blunt. I am astonish'd! What said he?

Lucy. Speechless he stood; but in his face

you might have read that various passions tore 120
his very soul. Oft he, in anguish, threw his eyes
towards Heaven, and then as often bent their
beams on her; then wept and groan'd, and beat
his breast; at length, with horror, not to be express'd, he cry'd: 'Thou cursed Fair! have I not 125
given dreadful proofs of love! What drew me
from my youthful innocence, to stain my then
unspotted soul, but love? What caus'd me to
rob my gentle master but cursed love? What
makes me now a fugitive from his service, loath'd 130
by my self, and scorn'd by all the world, but
love? What fills my eyes with tears, my soul
with torture, never felt on this side death before?
Why, love, love, love! And why, above all, do
I resolve' (for, tearing his hair, he cry'd 'I do re- 135
solve') 'to kill my uncle?'

Blunt. Was she not mov'd? It makes me
weep to hear the sad relation.

Lucy. Yes, with joy, that she had gain'd her
point. She gave him no time to cool, but urg'd 140
him to attempt it instantly. He's now gone; if
he performs it, and escapes, there's more money
for her; if not, he'll ne'er return, and then she's
fairly rid of him.

---

124 *his breast.* O4, O7, his troubled breast.
129 *my gentle.* O4, O7, my worthy gentle.
131 *by my self.* O7 only, by himself.

Blunt. 'Tis time the world was rid of such a 145 monster.

Lucy. If we don't do our endeavours to prevent this murder, we are as bad as she.

Blunt. I'm afraid it is too late.

Lucy. Perhaps not.—Her barbarity to Barn- 150 well makes me hate her. We've run too great a length with her already. I did not think her or my self so wicked, as I find, upon reflection, we are.

Blunt. 'Tis true, we have all been too much 155 so. But there is something so horrid in murder, that all other crimes seem nothing when compared to that. I wou'd not be involv'd in the guilt of that for all the world.

Lucy. Nor I, Heaven knows ; therefore, let us 160 clear our selves by doing all that is in our power to prevent it. I have just thought of a way that, to me, seems probable. Will you join with me to detect this curs'd design ?

Blunt. With all my heart.—How else shall I 165 clear my self ? He who knows of a murder intended to be committed and does not discover it, in the eye of the law and reason is a murderer.

Lucy. Let us lose no time ; I'll acquaint you 170 with the particulars as we go.　　　[*Exeunt.*]

145 *was rid.*　O7, were rid.
165–166 *How . . . my self.* O4, O7, omit.

Scene V.

A Walk at some distance from a Country Seat.

[Enter] Barnwell.

Barnwell. A dismal gloom obscures the face of day; either the sun has slip'd behind a cloud, or journeys down the west of Heaven, with more than common speed, to avoid the sight of what I'm doom'd to act. Since I set forth on this accursed design, where'er I tread, methinks, the solid earth trembles beneath my feet.—Yonder limpid stream, whose hoary fall has made a natural cascade, as I pass'd by, in doleful accents seem'd to murmur 'Murder.' The earth, the air, and water, seem concern'd—but that's not strange: the world is punish'd, and nature feels the shock, when Providence permits a good man's fall!—Just Heaven! Then what shou'd I be! For him, that was my father's only brother, and since his death has been to me a father, who took me up an infant, and an orphan; rear'd me with tenderest care, and still indulged me with most paternal fondness—yet here I stand avow'd his destin'd murderer.—I stiffen with horror at my own impiety.—'Tis yet unperform'd. What if I quit my bloody purpose, and fly the place! (*Going, then stops.*)—But

5

10

15

20

whither, O whither, shall I fly? My master's
once friendly doors are ever shut against me; 25
and without money Millwood will never see me
more, and life is not to be endured without her.
She's got such firm possession of my heart, and
governs there with such despotick sway—aye,
there's the cause of all my sin and sorrow! 'Tis 30
more than love: 'tis the fever of the soul, and
madness of desire. In vain does nature, reason,
conscience, all oppose it; the impetuous passion
bears down all before it, and drives me on to
lust, to theft and murder. Oh conscience! 35
feeble guide to virtue, who only shows us when
we go astray, but wants the power to stop us
in our course.—Ha, in yonder shady walk I see
my uncle. He's alone. Now for my disguise!
(*Plucks out a vizor.*) This is his hour of private 40
meditation. Thus daily he prepares his soul for
Heaven, whilst I—but what have I to do with
Heaven? Ha! No struggles, conscience!

Hence, hence, remorse, and ev'ry thought that's
good:
The storm that lust began must end in blood. 45
      Puts on the vizor, draws a pistol [and
      exit].

24 *whither, O whither,* O7, 1810. O1, O4, whether, O whether.
36 *who only shows us,* O1, O4. O7, thou only shows't.
37 *wants,* O1, O4. O7, wantest.
  and exit, O4, O7, 1810.

Scene VI.

A close Walk in a Wood.

[Enter] Uncle.

[*Uncle.*] If I was superstitious, I shou'd fear
some danger lurk'd unseen, or death were nigh.
—A heavy melancholy clouds my spirits; my
imagination is fill'd with gashly forms of dreary
graves and bodies chang'd by death; when the   5
pale, lengthen'd visage attracks each weeping eye,
and fills the musing soul, at once, with grief
and horror, pity and aversion.—I will indulge
the thought. The wise man prepares himself
for death, by making it familiar to his mind.   10
When strong reflections hold the mirror near,
and the living in the dead behold their future
selves, how does each inordinate passion and
desire cease, or sicken at the view? The mind
scarce moves; the blood, curdling and chill'd,   15
creeps slowly thro' the veins; fix'd, still, and motionless, like the solemn object of our thoughts,
we are almost at present what we must be hereafter, 'till curiosity awakes the soul, and sets it
on inquiry.   20

1 *was superstitious.* O4, O7, were.
4 *gashly*, O4 also. O7, 1775, 1810, ghastly.
6 *attracks.* O4, attacks; O7, attracts.
16-17 *motionless, like*, O1. O4, O7, motionless we stand, so
like.

Scene VII.

Uncle. George Barnwell at a distance.

Uncle. O Death, thou strange mysterious power,—seen every day, yet never understood but by the incommunicative dead—what art thou? The extensive mind of man, that with a thought circles the earth's vast globe, sinks to 5 the centre, or ascends above the stars; that worlds exotick finds, or thinks it finds—thy thick clouds attempts to pass in vain, lost and bewilder'd in the horrid gloom; defeated, she returns more doubtful than before; of nothing 10 certain but of labour lost.

> *During this speech, Barnwell sometimes presents the pistol and draws it back again; at last he drops it, at which his uncle starts, and draws his sword.*

Barnwell. Oh, 'tis impossible!

Uncle. A man so near me, arm'd and masqu'd!

Barn. Nay, then there's no retreat.

> *Plucks a poniard from his bosom, and stabs him.*

Uncle. Oh! I am slain! All-gracious Heaven 15 regard the prayer of thy dying servant! Bless,

7 *worlds*, O7. O1, 1775, 1810, world's.

8 *attempts*, O4, O7 also. 1775, 1810, attempt.

12 *Oh, 'tis impossible.* O4, O7, dropping the stage-direction from *at last* insert here: 'throwing down the pistol. Uncle starts and draws his sword.'

with thy choicest blessings, my dearest nephew ;
forgive my murderer, and take my fleeting soul
to endless mercy !

> *Barnwell throws off his mask, runs to him,
> and, kneeling by him, raises and chafes
> him.*

Barn. Expiring saint ! Oh, murder'd, martyr'd 20
uncle ! Lift up your dying eyes, and view your
nephew in your murderer ! O, do not look so
tenderly upon me ! Let indignation lighten from
your eyes, and blast me e're you die !—By
Heaven, he weeps in pity of my woes. Tears, 25
—tears, for blood ! The murder'd, in the agonies of death, weeps for his murderer.—Oh, speak
your pious purpose — pronounce my pardon
then—and take me with you !—He wou'd, but
cannot. O why with such fond affection do you 30
press my murdering hand !—What ! will you
kiss me ! (*Kisses him. Uncle groans and dies.*)
He's gone for ever—and oh ! I follow. (*Swoons
away upon his uncle's dead body.*) Do I still live to
press the suffering bosom of the earth ? Do I 35
still breathe, and taint with my infectious breath
the wholesome air ! Let Heaven from its high

Uncle groans and dies. After this stage-direction, O4, 1775,
and 1810 insert : ' Life, that hover'd on his lips but till he had seal'd
my pardon, in that sigh expired.' O7 substitutes ' kiss ' for sigh.
O1 misprints : *Uncle.* Groans and dies, — as if the last three words
were part of the dialogue.

throne, in justice or in mercy, now look down
on that dear murder'd saint, and me the murderer. And, if his vengeance spares, let pity 40
strike and end my wretched being!——Murder
the worst of crimes, and parricide the worst of
murders, and this the worst of parricides! Cain,
who stands on record from the birth of time,
and must to its last final period, as accurs'd, 45
slew a brother, favour'd above him. Detested
Nero by another's hand dispatch'd a mother
that he fear'd and hated. But I, with my own
hand, have murder'd a brother, mother, father,
and a friend, most loving and belov'd. This ex- 50
ecrable act of mine's without a parallel. O may
it ever stand alone—the last of murders, as it is
the worst!

The rich man thus, in torment and despair,
Prefer'd his vain, but charitable prayer. 55
The fool, his own soul lost, wou'd fain be wise
For others good ; but Heaven his suit denies.
By laws and means well known we stand or fall,
And one eternal rule remains for all.

The End of the Third Act.

Act IV.

Maria.

Maria. How falsely do they judge who censure or applaud as we're afflicted or rewarded here! I know I am unhappy, yet cannot charge my self with any crime, more than the common frailties of our kind, that shou'd provoke just 5 Heaven to mark me out for sufferings so uncommon and severe. Falsely to accuse our selves, Heaven must abhor; then it is just and right that innocence should suffer, for Heaven must be just in all its ways. Perhaps by that they are 10 kept from moral evils much worse than penal, or more improv'd in virtue; or may not the lesser ills that they sustain be the means of greater good to others? Might all the joyless days and sleepless nights that I have past but purchase 15 peace for thee—

Thou dear, dear cause of all my grief and pain,
Small were the loss, and infinite the gain;
Tho' to the grave in secret love I pine,
So life, and fame, and happiness were thine. 20

10, *they,* O4 also. O7, *we.*   13, *be the.* O4, O7, be made the.

Scene II.

[*Enter Trueman.*]
Trueman and Maria

Maria. What news of Barnwell?

Trueman. None. I have sought him with the greatest diligence, but all in vain.

Ma. Doth my father yet suspect the cause of his absenting himself?   5

True. All appear'd so just and fair to him, it is not possible he ever shou'd; but his absence will no longer be conceal'd. Your father's wise; and, though he seems to hearken to the friendly excuses I wou'd make for Barnwell, yet, I am   10 afraid, he regards 'em only as such, without suffering them to influence his judgment.

Ma. How does the unhappy youth defeat all our designs to serve him! Yet I can never repent what we have done. Shou'd he return, 'twill   15 make his reconciliation with my father easier, and preserve him from future reproach from a malicious, unforgiving world.

Scene III.

To them Thorowgood and Lucy.

Thorowgood. This woman here has given me a sad, and (bating some circumstances) too probable account of Barnwell's defection.

4 *Doth*, O4, O7, Does.   5 *absenting himself.* O4, O7, absence.

Lucy. I am sorry, sir, that my frank confession of my former unhappy course of life shou'd cause you to suspect my truth on this occasion. 5

Thor. It is not that; your confession has in it all the appearance of truth. (*To them.*) Among many other particulars, she informs me that Barnwell has been influenc'd to break his trust, 10 and wrong me, at several times, of considerable sums of money; now, as I know this to be false, I wou'd fain doubt the whole of her relation, too dreadful to be willingly believ'd.

Maria. Sir, your pardon; I find my self on a 15 sudden so indispos'd, that I must retire.—(*Aside.*) Providence opposes all attempts to save him. Poor ruin'd Barnwell! Wretched, lost Maria!

[*Exit.*]

Scene IV.

Thorowgood, Trueman and Lucy.

Thorowgood. How am I distress'd on every side? Pity for that unhappy youth, fear for the life of a much valued friend — and then my child, the only joy and hope of my declining life! Her melancholy increases hourly, and gives 5 me painful apprehensions of her loss.—O Trueman! this person informs me that your friend, at the instigation of an impious woman, is gone to rob and murder his venerable uncle.

Trueman. O execrable deed! I am blasted 10
with the horror of the thought.

Lucy. This delay may ruin all.

Thor. What to do or think I know not. That
he ever wrong'd me, I know is false; the rest
may be so too—there's all my hope.   15

True. Trust not to that; rather suppose all
true than lose a moment's time. Even now the
horrid deed may be a doing—dreadful imagination! Or it may be done, and we are vainly
debating on the means to prevent what is already 20
past.

Thor. [*aside*]. This earnestness convinces me
that he knows more than he has yet discover'd.
—— What ho! without there! who waits?

Scene V.

To them a Servant.

Thorowgood. Order the groom to saddle the
swiftest horse, and prepare himself to set out
with speed!——An affair of life and death demands
his diligence.   [*Exit Servant.*]

Scene VI.

Thorowgood, Trueman and Lucy.

Thorowgood. For you, whose behaviour on this
occasion I have no time to commend as it de-

Sc. V.   2 *himself.* O4, O7, omit.

serves, I must ingage your farther assistance.
Return and observe this Millwood till I come.
I have your directions, and will follow you as   5
soon as possible.   [*Exit Lucy.*]

Scene VII.

Thorowgood and Trueman.

Thorowgood. Trueman, you I am sure wou'd
not be idle on this occasion.   [*Exit.*]

Scene VIII.

Trueman.

[*Trueman.*] He only who is a friend can judge
of my distress.   [*Exit.*]

Scene IX.

Millwood's House.

Millwood.

Millwood. I wish I knew the event of his design; the attempt without success would ruin
him.—Well! what have I to apprehend from
that? I fear too much. The mischief being
only intended, his friends, in pity of his youth, 5
turn all their rage on me. I shou'd have thought
of that before.—Suppose the deed done: then,
and then only, I shall be secure; or what if he
returns without attempting it at all?

Sc. VII. 1–2 *wou'd not.* O7, will not.

Scene X.

Millwood, and [enter] Barnwell, bloody.

Millwood. But he is here, and I have done him wrong; his bloody hands show he has done the deed, but show he wants the prudence to conceal it.

Barnwell. Where shall I hide me? whither 5
shall I fly to avoid the swift, unerring hand of justice?

Mill. Dismiss those fears: tho' thousands had pursu'd you to the door, yet being enter'd here you are safe as innocence. I have such 10
a cavern, by art so cunningly contriv'd, that the piercing eyes of jealousy and revenge may search in vain, nor find the entrance to the safe retreat. There will I hide you, if any danger's near. 15

Barn. O hide me from my self, if it be possible; for while I bear my conscience in my bosom, tho' I were hid, where man's eye never saw, nor light e'er dawned, 'twere all in vain. For that inmate,—that impartial judge, will try, 20
convict and sentence me for murder; and exe-

enter Barnwell. 1810 makes Barnwell enter at the close of Millwood's speech.

5 *whither,* O7, 1775, 1810. O1, whether.
8 *those.* O4, O7, your.
20 *For that.* O4, O7, For oh! that.

cute me with never ending torments. Behold
these hands all crimson'd o'er with my dear
uncle's blood! Here's a sight to make a statue
start with horror, or turn a living man into a 25
statue.

Mill. Ridiculous! Then, it seems you are
afraid of your own shadow, or, what's less than
a shadow, your conscience.

Barn. Though to man unknown I did the 30
accursed act, what can we hide from Heav'ns
omniscient eye?

Mill. No more of this stuff! What advantage have you made of his death? or what advantage may yet be made of it? Did you secure 35
the keys of his treasure—those no doubt were
about him. What gold, what jewels, or what
else of value have you brought me?

Barn. Think you I added sacrilege to murder? Oh! had you seen him as his life flowed 40
from him in a crimson flood, and heard him
praying for me by the double name of nephew
and of murderer—alas, alas! he knew not then
that his nephew was his murderer: how wou'd
you have wish'd, as I did, tho' you had a thou- 45
sand years of life to come, to have given them
all to have lengthen'd his one hour! But being
dead, I fled the sight of what my hands had done,

32 *omniscient.* O4, O7, all-seeing.

nor cou'd I, to have gain'd the empire of the
world, have violated by theft his sacred corps.   50

Mill. Whining, preposterous, canting villain,
to murder your uncle, rob him of life, natures
first, last, dear prerogative, after which there's
no injury, then fear to take what he no longer
wanted; and bring to me your penury and guilt!   55
Do you think I'll hazard my reputation; nay
my life to entertain you?

Barn. Oh! Millwood! this from thee! —
but I have done — if you hate me, if you wish
me dead: then are you happy — for oh! 'tis   60
sure my grief will quickly end me.

Mill. In his madness he will discover all, and
involve me in his ruin. We are on a precipice
from whence there's no retreat for both—then,
to preserve my self. (*Pauses.*) There is no   65
other way, — 'tis dreadful; but reflection comes
too late when danger's pressing, and there's no
room for choice. — It must be done.   (*Stamps.*)

SCENE XI.

To them a Servant.

Millwood. Fetch me an officer, and scize this
villain: he has confess'd himself a murderer.

68 *It must be done.* Here, instead of *Stamps* (which is also the
stage-direction in 1810), O4 has *Rings a bell;* and O7, 1775
have the direction : *Aside. Rings a bell. Enter a Servant.*

Shou'd I let him escape, I justly might be thought as bad as he.   [*Exit Servant.*]

Scene XII.

Millwood and Barnwell.

Barnwell. O Millwood! sure thou dost not, cannot mean it. Stop the messenger, upon my knees I beg you, call him back! 'Tis fit I die indeed, but not by you. I will this instant deliver my self into the hands of justice; indeed I 5 will, for death is all I wish. But thy ingratitude so tears my wounded soul, 'tis worse ten thousand times than death with torture.

Millwood. Call it what you will, I am willing to live, and live secure; which nothing but your 10 death can warrant.

Barn. If there be a pitch of wickedness that seats the author beyond the reach of vengeance, you must be secure. But what remains for me but a dismal dungeon, hard-galling fetters, an 15 awful tryal, and ignominious death—justly to fall unpitied and abhorr'd; after death to be suspended between Heaven and earth, a dreadful spectacle, the warning and horror of a gaping croud. This I cou'd bear, nay wish not to 20 avoid, had it come from any hand but thine.

    1 *thou dost not,* O1. O4, O7, you do not.
    3 *beg you, call.* O4, O7, beg you'd call.
  16 *and ignominious.* O7, and an ignominious.

SCENE XIII.

Millwood, Barnwell. [*Enter*] *Blunt, Officer and Attendants.*

Millwood. Heaven defend me! Conceal a murderer! Here, sir; take this youth into your custody. I accuse him of murder, and will appear to make good my charge.   *They seize him.*

Barnwell. To whom, of what, or how shall 5
I complain? I'll not accuse her: the hand of Heav'n is in it, and this the punishment of lust and parricide. Yet Heav'n, that justly cuts me off, still suffers her to live, perhaps to punish others. Tremendous mercy! so fiends are curs'd 10
with immortality, to be the executioners of Heaven.——

Be warn'd, ye youths, who see my sad despair,
Avoid lewd women, false as they are fair;
By reason guided, honest joys pursue;   15
The fair, to honour and to virtue true,
Just to her self, will ne'er be false to you.
By my example learn to shun my fate;
(How wretched is the man who's wise too late!)
E'er innocence, and fame, and life, be lost,   20
Here purchase wisdom, cheaply, at my cost!
                    [*Exit with Officers.*]

16 *The fair, to honour and.* All the editions interpunctuate:
The fair to honour, and.

Scene XIV.

Millwood and Blunt.

Millwood. Where's Lucy? Why is she absent at such a time?

Blunt. Wou'd I had been so too, thou devil!

Mill. Insolent! This to me!

Blunt. The worst that we know of the devil   5
is, that he first seduces to sin and then betrays
to punishment.   [*Exit.*]

Scene XV.

Millwood.

[*Millwood.*] They disapprove of my conduct,
and mean to take this opportunity to set up for
themselves. My ruin is resolv'd. I see my
danger, but scorn it and them. I was not born
to fall by such weak instruments.   *Going.*   5

Scene XVI.

[*Enter Thorowgood.*]

Thorowgood and Millwood.

Thorowgood. Where is this scandal of her own
sex, and curse of ours?

Sc. XIV. 3 *so too.* Here O4, O7, 1775, 1810, insert : Lucy
will soon be here, and I hope to thy confusion.

Sc. XV. 1 *conduct.* O4, O7, add, then.

Sc. XVI. 1 *this scandal.* O4, O7, the scandal.

Millwood. What means this insolence? Who do you seek?

Thor. Millwood.   5

Mill. Well, you have found her, then. I am Millwood.

Thor. Then you are the most impious wretch that e'er the sun beheld.

Mill. From your appearance I shou'd have 10
expected wisdom and moderation, but your manners bely your aspect.—What is your business here? I know you not.

Thor. Hereafter you may know me better; I am Barnwell's master.   15

Mill. Then you are master to a villain; which, I think, is not much to your credit.

Thor. Had he been as much above thy arts as my credit is superior to thy malice, I need not blush to own him.   20

Mill. My arts? I don't understand you, sir. If he has done amiss, what's that to me? Was he my servant, or yours? You shou'd have taught him better.

Thor. Why shou'd I wonder to find such 25
uncommon impudence in one arriv'd to such a height of wickedness? When innocence is banish'd, modesty soon follows. Know, sorceress, I'm not ignorant of any of your arts, by which

you first deceiv'd the unwary youth. I know 30
how, step by step, you've led him on, reluctant
and unwilling from crime to crime, to this last
horrid act, which you contriv'd, and, by your
curs'd wiles, even forced him to commit—and
then betray'd him. 35

Mill. (*aside*). Ha! Lucy has got the advantage of me, and accused me first. Unless I can
turn the accusation, and fix it upon her and
Blunt, I am lost.

Thor. Had I known your cruel design sooner, 40
it had been prevented. To see you punish'd as
the law directs, is all that now remains.—Poor
satisfaction—for he, innocent as he is, compared to you, must suffer too. But Heaven,
who knows our frame, and graciously distin- 45
guishes between frailty and presumption, will
make a difference, tho' man cannot, who sees
not the heart, but only judges by the outward
action.—

Mill. I find, sir, we are both unhappy in our 50
servants. I was surpriz'd at such ill treatment
from a gentleman of your appearance, without
cause, and therefore too hastily return'd it; for
which I ask your pardon. I now perceive you

34–35 *and . . . him.* O4, O7, omit.

37 *of me.* O4, O7, omit.

52–53 *without cause.* O4, O7, 1775, transpose these words to
after *ill treatment.*

have been so far impos'd on as to think me 55
engaged in a former correspondence with your
servant, and, some way or other, accessary to
his undoing.

Thor. I charge you as the cause, the sole
cause of all his guilt and all his suffering — of 60
all he now endures, and must endure, till a violent and shameful death shall put a dreadful
period to his life and miseries together.

Mill. 'Tis very strange! But who's secure
from scandal and detraction? — So far from 65
contributing to his ruin, I never spoke to him
till since that fatal accident, which I lament as
much as you. 'Tis true, I have a servant, on
whose account he has of late frequented my
house; if she has abus'd my good opinion of 70
her, am I to blame? Hasn't Barnwell done the
same by you?

Thor. I hear you; pray, go on!

Mill. I have been inform'd he had a violent
passion for her, and she for him; but I always 75
thought it innocent; I know her poor, and given
to expensive pleasures. Now who can tell but
she may have influenced the amorous youth to
commit this murder, to supply her extravagan-
cies? It must be so; I now recollect a thousand 80
circumstances that confirm it. I'll have her and

75 *but.* O4, O7 insert, till now.

a man-servant, that I suspect as an accomplice, secured immediately. I hope, sir, you will lay aside your ill-grounded suspicions of me, and join to punish the real contrivers of this bloody 85 deed. *Offers to go.*

Thor. Madam, you pass not this way! I see your design, but shall protect them from your malice.

Mill. I hope you will not use your influence, 90 and the credit of your name, to skreen such guilty wretches. Consider, sir, the wickedness of perswading a thoughtless youth to such a crime!

Thor. I do — and of betraying him when it 95 was done.

Mill. That which you call betraying him, may convince you of my innocence. She who loves him, tho' she contriv'd the murder, would never have deliver'd him into the hands of justice, as I, 100 struck with the horror of his crimes, have done.

Thor. [*aside*]. How shou'd an unexperienc'd youth escape her snares? The powerful magick of her wit and form might betray the wisest to simple dotage, and fire the blood that age had 105 froze long since. Even I, that with just prejudice came prepared, had, by her artful story, been deceiv'd, but that my strong conviction of her guilt

101 *with the horror of.* O4, O7, with horror at.

makes even a doubt impossible.—Those whom
subtilly you wou'd accuse, you know are your 110
accusers; and, what proves unanswerably their
innocence and your guilt, they accus'd you before the deed was done, and did all that was in
their power to have prevented it.

Mill. Sir, you are very hard to be convinc'd; 115
but I have such a proof, which, when produced,
will silence all objections.   [*Exit.*]

Scene XVII.

Thorowgood. [*Enter*] *Lucy, Trueman, Blunt,*
Officers, etc.

Lucy. Gentlemen, pray, place your selves,
some on one side of that door, and some on
the other; watch her entrance, and act as your
prudence shall direct you—this way! (*to Thor-*
owgood) and note her behaviour. I have ob-   5
serv'd her: she's driven to the last extremity,
and is forming some desperate resolution.—I
guess at her design.—

Scene XVIII.

To them Millwood with a pistol.—Trueman
secures her.

Trueman. Here thy power of doing mischief
ends, deceitful, cruel, bloody woman!

111 *and, what,* O4 also. O7, *and* (*which proves.*
114 *have prevented,* O4 also. O7, *prevent.*

Millwood. Fool, hypocrite, villain — man! Thou can'st not call me that.

True. To call thee woman were to wrong the sex, thou devil!

Mill. That imaginary being is an emblem of thy cursed sex collected — a mirrour, wherein each particular man may see his own likeness, and that of all mankind.

True. Think not by aggravating the fault of others to extenuate thy own, of which the abuse of such uncommon perfections of mind and body is not the least!

Mill. If such I had, well may I curse your barbarous sex, who robb'd me of 'em, e'er I knew their worth, then left me, too late, to count their value by their loss. Another and another spoiler came; and all my gain was poverty and reproach. My soul disdain'd, and yet disdains, dependance and contempt. Riches, no matter by what means obtain'd, I saw, secur'd the worst of men from both; I found it therefore necessary to be rich; and, to that end, I summon'd all my arts. You call 'em wicked; be it so! They were such as my conversation with your sex had furnish'd me withal.

Thorowgood. Sure, none but the worst of men convers'd with thee.

6 *the sex.* O4, O7, thy sex.

Mill. Men of all degrees and all professions 30
I have known, yet found no difference, but in
their several capacities; all were alike wicked to
the utmost of their power. In pride, contention,
avarice, cruelty and revenge, the reverend priest-
hood were my unerring guides. From suburb- 35
magistrates, who live by ruin'd reputations, as
the unhospitable natives of Cornwall do by ship-
wrecks, I learn'd that to charge my innocent
neighbours with my crimes, was to merit their
protection; for to skreen the guilty is the less 40
scandalous, when many are suspected, and detraction, like darkness and death, blackens all
objects and levels all distinction. Such are your
venal magistrates, who favour none but such as,
by their office, they are sworn to punish. With 45
them, not to be guilty is the worst of crimes; and
large fees privately paid is every needful virtue.

Thor. Your practice has sufficiently discover'd
your contempt of laws, both human and divine;
no wonder then that you shou'd hate the officers 50
of both.

Mill. I hate you all; I know you, and expect no mercy. Nay, I ask for none; I have
done nothing that I am sorry for; I follow'd my

47 *is.* O7, 1810, are.
52–53 *I hate . . . for none.* O4, O7, I know you, and I
hate you all; I expect no mercy, and I ask for none.
53–54 *I have . . . sorry for.* O4, O7, omit.

inclinations, and that the best of you does every 55
day. All actions are alike natural and indifferent
to man and beast, who devour, or are devour'd,
as they meet with others weaker or stronger
than themselves.

Thor. What pity   a mind so comprehen- 60
sive, daring and inquis.   be a stranger
to religion's sweet, bu   harms.

Mill. I am not fool en   be an atheist,
tho' I have known enoug   ens hypocrisy
to make a thousand simple   n so. What- 65
ever religion is in it self—as practis'd by mankind, it has caus'd the evils you say it was design'd to cure. War, plague, and famine, has
not destroy'd so many of the human race as this
pretended piety has done, and with such bar- 70
barous cruelty—as if the only way to honour
Heaven, were to turn the present world into
Hell.

Thor. Truth is truth, tho' from an enemy
and spoke in malice. You bloody, blind, and 75
superstitious bigots, how will you answer this?

Mill. What are your laws, of which you
make your boast, but the fool's wisdom, and the
coward's valour; the instrument and skreen of
all your villanies, by which you punish in others 80

55 *does.* O4, O7, do.   56 *are.* O4, O7, seem.
62 *but.* O4, O7, and.   68–69 *has not.* O7, have not.

what you act your selves, or wou'd have acted,
had you been in their circumstances. The judge
who condemns the poor man for being a thief,
had been a thief himself, had he been poor. Thus
you go on deceiving, and being deceiv'd, har- 85
rassing, and plaguing, and destroying one another : but women are your universal prey.

Women, by whom you are, the source of joy,
With cruel arts you labour to destroy ;
A thousand ways our ruin you pursue, 90
Yet blame in us those arts first taught by you.
O may, from hence, each violated maid,
By flatt'ring, faithless, barb'rous man betray'd,
When robb'd of innocence, and virgin fame,
From your destruction raise a nobler name ; 95
To right their sex's wrongs devote their mind,
And future Millwoods prove, to plague mankind!

88 *by whom you are, etc.* 1775 absurdly omits the comma, and
reads : *by whom you are the source of joy.*

The End of the Fourth Act.

Act V.

Scene I. *A Room in a Prison.*

Thorowgood, Blunt and Lucy.

Thorowgood. I have recommended to Barnwell
a reverend divine, whose judgment and integrity I am well acquainted with. Nor has Millwood been neglected; but she, unhappy woman,
still obstinate, refuses his assistance.   5

Lucy. This pious charity to the afflicted well
becomes your character; yet pardon me, sir, if
I wonder you were not at their trial.

Thor. I knew it was impossible to save him,
and I and my family bear so great a part in his   10
distress, that to have been present wou'd have
aggravated our sorrows without relieving his.

Blunt. It was mournful indeed. Barnwell's
youth and modest deportment, as he past, drew
tears from every eye: when placed at the bar,   15
and arraigned before the reverend judges, with
many tears and interrupting sobs he confess'd
and aggravated his offences, without accusing,
or once reflecting on Millwood, the shameless
author of his ruin; who dauntless and uncon-   20
cern'd stood by his side, viewing with visible

11 *wou'd have*, O4 also. O7, wou'd but have.

pride and contempt the vast assembly, who all
with sympathizing sorrow wept for the wretched
youth. Millwood, when called upon to answer,
loudly insisted upon her innocence, and made 25
an artful and a bold defence; but, finding all in
vain, the impartial jury and the learned bench
concurring to find her guilty, how did she curse
her self, poor Barnwell, us, her judges, all mankind! But what cou'd that avail? She was con- 30
demn'd, and is this day to suffer with him.

Thor. The time draws on. I am going to
visit Barnwell, as you are Millwood.

Lucy. We have not wrong'd her, yet I dread
this interview. She's proud, impatient, wrathful, 35
and unforgiving. To be the branded instruments
of vengeance, to suffer in her shame, and sym-
pathize with her in all she suffers, is the tribute
we must pay for our former ill-spent lives, and
long confederacy with her in wickedness. 40

Thor. Happy for you it ended when it did!
What you have done against Millwood, I know,
proceeded from a just abhorrence of her crimes,
free from interest, malice, or revenge. Prose-
lytes to virtue shou'd be encourag'd. Pursue 45
your proposed reformation, and know me hereafter for your friend.

Lucy. This is a blessing as unhop'd for as
unmerited; but Heaven, that snatched us from

impending ruin, sure, intends you as its instru- 50
ment to secure us from apostacy.

Thor. With gratitude to impute your deliverance to Heaven is just. Many, less virtuously
dispos'd than Barnwell was, have never fallen
in the manner he has done ;—may not such owe 55
their safety rather to Providence than to themselves ? With pity and compassion let us judge
him ! Great were his faults, but strong was
the temptation. Let his ruin learn us diffidence,
humanity and circumspection ; for we, who 60
wonder at his fate—perhaps, had we like him
been tryed, like him we had fallen too.

[*Exeunt.*]

Scene II.

A Dungeon. A table and lamp.

Barnwell, reading. [Enter] Thorowgood.

Thorowgood. See there the bitter fruits of passion's detested reign and sensual appetite in-
dulg'd—severe reflections, penitence and tears.

Barnwell. My honoured, injured master,
whose goodness has covered me a thousand times 5
with shame, forgive this last unwilling disre-
spect ! Indeed, I saw you not.

Thor. 'Tis well ; I hope you were better im-

1 *See there*, O1. O4, O7, add to [*Enter*] *Thorowgood :* 'at a
distance.' O7, There see.

ploy'd in viewing of your self. Your journey's
long, your time for preparation almost spent. I 10
sent a reverend divine to teach you to improve
it, and shou'd be glad to hear of his success.

Barn. The word of truth, which he recommended for my constant companion in this my
sad retirement, has at length remov'd the doubts 15
I labour'd under. From thence I've learn'd the
infinite extent of heavenly mercy ; that my offences, tho' great, are not unpardonable ; and
that 'tis not my interest only, but my duty, to
believe and to rejoice in that hope : so shall 20
Heaven receive the glory, and future penitents
the profit of my example.

Thor. Go on ! How happy am I who live to
see this !

Barn. 'Tis wonderful that words shou'd 25
charm despair, speak peace and pardon to a
murderer's conscience ! But truth and mercy
flow in every sentence attended with force and
energy divine. How shall I describe my present
state of mind ? I hope in doubt, and trembling 30
I rejoice. I feel my grief increase, even as my
fears give way. Joy and gratitude now supply
more tears than the horror and anguish of despair before.

Thor. These are the genuine signs of true 35

23–24 *Go on . . . see this.* O4, O7, Proceed.

repentance, the only preparatory certain way
to everlasting peace.—O the joy it gives to see
a soul form'd and prepar'd for Heaven! For
this the faithful minister devotes himself to
meditation, abstinence and prayer, shunning the 40
vain delights of sensual joys, and daily dies, that
others may live for ever. For this he turns the
sacred volumes o'er, and spends his life in painful search of truth. The love of riches and the
lust of power he looks on with just contempt 45
and detestation, who only counts for wealth the
souls he wins, and whose highest ambition is to
serve mankind. If the reward of all his pains
be to preserve one soul from wandering, or turn
one from the error of his ways, how does he 50
then rejoice, and own his little labours over
paid!

Barn. What do I owe for all your generous
kindness? But, tho' I cannot, Heaven can and
will reward you. 55

Thor. To see thee thus is joy too great for
words. Farewell! Heaven strengthen thee!
Farewell!

Barn. O, sir, there's something I cou'd say,
if my sad swelling heart would give me leave. 60

Thor. Give it vent a while, and try.

36 *preparatory certain.* O4, O7, preparatory the certain.
45 *looks on.* O4, O7, looks upon.
59 *I cou'd say.* O4, O7, I would say.

Barn. I had a friend—'tis true I am unworthy, yet methinks your generous example
might perswade—cou'd I not see him once before I go from whence there's no return?   65

Thor. He's coming, and as much thy friend
as ever; but I'll not anticipate his sorrow: too
soon he'll see the sad effect of this contagious
ruin.—[*Aside.*] This torrent of domestick misery bears too hard upon me; I must retire to 70
indulge a weakness I find impossible to overcome.—Much lov'd and much lamented youth,
farewell! Heaven strengthen thee! Eternally
farewell!

Barn. The best of masters and of men, fare- 75
well! While I live, let me not want your
prayers!

Thor. Thou shalt not. Thy peace being
made with Heaven, death's already vanquish'd;
bear a little longer the pains that attend this 80
transitory life, and cease from pain for ever.

[*Exit.*]

Scene III.

Barnwell.

Barnwell. I find a power within that bears
my soul above the fears of death, and, spight of
conscious shame and guilt, gives me a taste of
pleasure more than mortal.

68 *this contagious.* O1, his contagious. O4 corrects.
 1 *I find.* O4, O7, prefix: Perhaps I shall.

Scene IV.

To him Trueman and Keeper.

Keeper. Sir, there's the prisoner. [*Exit.*]

Scene V.

Barnwell and Trueman.

Barnwell. Trueman—my friend, whom I so wisht to see! Yet now he's here I dare not look upon him. *Weeps.*

Trueman. Oh Barnwell! Barnwell!

Barn. Mercy, Mercy, gracious Heaven! For death, but not for this, was I prepared. 5

True. What have I suffer'd since I saw you last! What pain has absence given me!—But oh! to see thee thus!

Barn. I know it is dreadful! I feel the anguish of thy generous soul—but I was born to murder all who love me. *Both weep.* 10

True. I came not to reproach you; I thought to bring you comfort. But I'm deceiv'd, for I have none to give. I came to share thy sorrow, but cannot bear my own. 15

Barn. My sense of guilt indeed you cannot know—'tis what the good and innocent, like you, can ne'er conceive. But other griefs at present I have none, but what I feel for you. In your 20

6 *was I,* O4 also. O7, I was.   8 *has.* O4, O7, hath.

sorrow I read you love me still. But yet methinks 'tis strange, when I consider what I am.

True. No more of that! I can remember
nothing but thy virtues, thy honest, tender friendship, our former happy state, and present misery. 25
—O, had you trusted me when first the fair
seducer tempted you, all might have been prevented.

Barn. Alas, thou know'st not what a wretch
I've been! Breach of friendship was my first 30
and least offence. So far was I lost to goodness,
so devoted to the author of my ruin, that, had
she insisted on my murdering thee, I think I
shou'd have done it.

True. Prithee, aggravate thy faults no more! 35

Barn. I think I shou'd! Thus, good and
generous as you are, I shou'd have murder'd
you!

True. We have not yet embrac'd, and may be
interrupted. Come to my arms!   40

Barn. Never, never will I taste such joys on
earth; never will I so sooth my just remorse!
Are those honest arms and faithful bosom fit
to embrace and to support a murderer? These
iron fetters only shall clasp, and flinty pavement 45
bear me (*throwing himself on the ground*)—even
these too good for such a bloody monster.

True. Shall fortune sever those whom friend-

ship join'd? Thy miseries cannot lay thee so
low, but love will find thee. (*Lies down by him.*) 50
Upon this rugged couch then let us lie; for well
it suits our most deplorable condition. Here
will we offer to stern calamity, this earth the
altar, and our selves the sacrifice! Our mutual
groans shall eccho to each other thro' the dreary 55
vault. Our sighs shall number the moments as
they pass, and mingling tears communicate such
anguish as words were never made to express.

Barn. Then be it so! Since you propose an
intercourse of woe, pour all your griefs into my 60
breast, and in exchange take mine! (*Embracing.*)
Where's now the anguish that you promis'd?
You've taken mine, and make me no return.
Sure, peace and comfort dwell within these arms,
and sorrow can't approach me while I'm here! 65
This too is the work of Heaven, who, having
before spoke peace and pardon to me, now sends
thee to confirm it. O take, take some of the
joy that overflows my breast!

True. I do, I do. Almighty Power, how have 70
you made us capable to bear, at once, the ex-
treams of pleasure and of pain?

50 *Lies down by him.* O4, O7, omit this direction and the
sentence from *upon* to *condition.*

53 *this earth.* O4, O7, this place.

66 *Heaven, who.* O4, O7, Heaven, which.

70–71 *how have you made,* O4 also. O7, how hast thou made.

Scene VI.

To them, Keeper.

Keeper. Sir!

Trueman. I come.　　　　　　　[*Exit Keeper.*]

Scene VII.

Barnwell and Trueman.

Barnwell. Must you leave me? Death would soon have parted us for ever.

Trueman. O my Barnwell, there's yet another task behind; again your heart must bleed for others woes.　　　　　　　　　　　5

Barn. To meet and part with you, I thought was all I had to do on earth! What is there more for me to do or suffer?

True. I dread to tell thee; yet it must be known!—Maria—　　　　　　　　10

Barn. Our master's fair and virtuous daughter?

True. The same.

Barn. No misfortune, I hope, has reach'd that lovely maid! Preserve her, Heaven, from every 15 ill, to show mankind that goodness is your care!

True. Thy, thy misfortunes, my unhappy friend, have reach'd her. Whatever you and I have felt, and more, if more be possible, she feels for you.　　　　　　　　　　20

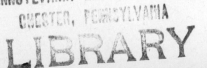

Barn. (*aside*). I know he doth abhor a lie, and would not trifle with his dying friend. This is, indeed, the bitterness of death!

True. You must remember, for we all observ'd it, for some time past, a heavy melancholy weigh'd her down. Disconsolate she seem'd, and pin'd and languish'd from a cause unknown;— till, hearing of your dreadful fate,—the long stifled flame blaz'd out. She wept, she wrung her hands, and tore her hair, and, in the transport of her grief, discover'd her own lost state, whilst she lamented yours.

Barn. Will all the pain I feel restore thy ease, lovely unhappy maid? (*Weeping.*) Why didn't you let me die and never know it?

True. It was impossible; she makes no secret of her passion for you, and is determin'd to see you e'er you die. She waits for me to introduce her. [*Exit.*]

Scene VIII.

Barnwell.

Barnwell. Vain, busy thoughts, be still! What avails it to think on what I might have been? I now am what I've made myself.

32 *whilst*, O4 also. O7, 1810, while.
35 *didn't*. O4, O7, did you not.

Scene IX.

To him, Trueman and Maria.

Trueman. Madam, reluctant I lead you to this
dismal scene. This is the seat of misery and
guilt. Here awful justice reserves her publick
victims. This is the entrance to shameful death.

Maria. To this sad place, then, no improper　5
guest, the abandon'd, lost Maria brings despair—
and see the subject and the cause of all this
world of woe! Silent and motionless he stands,
as if his soul had quitted her abode, and the
lifeless form alone was left behind—yet that so　10
perfect that beauty and death, ever at enmity,
now seem united there.

Barnwell. I groan, but murmur not. Just
Heaven, I am your own; do with me what you
please.　15

Ma. Why are your streaming eyes still fix'd
below, as tho' thoud'st give the greedy earth thy
sorrows, and rob me of my due? Were happiness within your power, you should bestow it
where you pleas'd; but in your misery I must　20
and will partake!

Barn. Oh! say not so, but fly, abhor, and
leave me to my fate! Consider what you are—
how vast your fortune, and how bright your
fame; have pity on your youth, your beauty,　25

and unequalled virtue, for which so many noble peers have sigh'd in vain! Bless with your charms some honourable lord! Adorn with your beauty, and by your example improve, the English court, that justly claims such merit: so shall I quickly 30 be to you as though I had never been.

Ma. When I forget you, I must be so indeed. Reason, choice, virtue, all forbid it. Let women, like Millwood, if there be more such women, smile in prosperity, and in adversity 35 forsake! Be it the pride of virtue to repair, or to partake, the ruin such have made.

True. Lovely, ill-fated maid! Was there ever such generous distress before? How must this pierce his grateful heart, and aggravate his 40 woes?

Barn. E'er I knew guilt or shame—when fortune smiled, and when my youthful hopes were at the highest—if then to have rais'd my thoughts to you, had been presumption in me, never to 45 have been pardon'd: think how much beneath your self you condescend, to regard me now!

Ma. Let her blush, who, professing love, invades the freedom of your sex's choice, and meanly sues in hopes of a return! Your inevit- 50 able fate hath render'd hope impossible as vain. Then, why shou'd I fear to avow a passion so just and so disinterested?

34 *there be*, O4 also. O7, there are.

True. If any shou'd take occasion, from Mill- 55
wood's crimes, to libel the best and fairest part
of the creation, here let them see their error!
The most distant hopes of such a tender passion
from so bright a maid might add to the happiness of the most happy, and make the greatest
proud. Yet here 'tis lavish'd in vain: tho' by 60
the rich present, the generous donor is undone,
he on whom it is bestow'd receives no benefit.

Barn. So the aromatick spices of the East,
which all the living covet and esteem, are, with
unavailing kindness, wasted on the dead. 65

Ma. Yes, fruitless is my love, and unavailing
all my sighs and tears. Can they save thee from
approaching death—from such a death? O,
terrible idea! What is her misery and distress,
who sees the first last object of her love, for 70
whom alone she'd live—for whom she'd die a
thousand, thousand deaths, if it were possible—
expiring in her arms? Yet she is happy, when
compar'd to me. Were millions of worlds mine,
I'd gladly give them in exchange for her con- 75
dition. The most consummate woe is light to
mine. The last of curses to other miserable
maids is all I ask; and that's deny'd me.

True. Time and reflection cure all ills.

Ma. All but this; his dreadful catastrophe 80

78 *I ask.* O4, O7, insert: for my relief.

virtue her self abhors. To give a holiday to
suburb slaves, and passing entertain the savage
herd, who, elbowing each other for a sight, pursue and press upon him like his fate! A mind
with piety and resolution arm'd may smile on 85
death. But publick ignominy, everlasting shame,
—shame, the death of souls—to die a thousand
times, and yet survive even death it self, in never
dying infamy—is this to be endured? Can I,
who live in him, and must, each hour of my 90
devoted life, feel all these woes renew'd, can I
endure this?

True. Grief has impair'd her spirits; she
pants as in the agonies of death.

Barn. Preserve her, Heaven, and restore her 95
peace; nor let her death be added to my crime!
(*Bell tolls.*) I am summon'd to my fate.

Scene X.

To them, Keeper.

Keeper. The officers attend you, sir. Mrs.
Millwood is already summon'd.

Barnwell. Tell 'em, I'm ready.—And now,
my friend, farewell! (*Embracing.*) Support and

93 *has impair'd.* O4, O7, has so impair'd.
96 *crime.* O4, O7, 1810, crimes.
 1 *The officers . . . sir.* O4, O7, place *sir* first.
 Mrs. O4, O7, omit.

comfort the best you can this mourning fair. 5
—No more! Forget not to pray for me!—
(*Turning to Maria.*) Would you, bright excellence, permit me the honour of a chaste embrace,
the last happiness this world cou'd give were
mine. (*She enclines toward him; they embrace.*) 10
Exalted goodness! O turn your eyes from earth,
and me, to Heaven, where virtue, like yours, is
ever heard. Pray for the peace of my departing
soul! Early my race of wickedness began, and
soon has reach'd the summet. E'er nature has 15
finish'd her work, and stamp'd me man—just at
the time that others begin to stray—my course
is finish'd. Tho' short my span of life, and few
my days, yet, count my crimes for years, and I
have liv'd whole ages. Justice and mercy are in 20
Heaven the same : its utmost severity is mercy
to the whole, thereby to cure man's folly and
presumption, which else wou'd render even infinite mercy vain and ineffectual. Thus justice,
in compassion to mankind, cuts off a wretch like 25
me, by one such example to secure thousands
from future ruin.

15 *soon has reach'd*, O4 also. O7, soon I reach'd.
20–21 *Justice and mercy are in Heaven the same.* In 1775 these
words are transposed to the end of Barnwell's speech, after *from
future ruin.* O4, O7, print *Justice . . . ineffectual* after *Thus
justice . . . ruin.*

If any youth, like you, in future times
Shall mourn my fate, tho' he abhor my crimes;
Or tender maid, like you, my tale shall hear,   30
And to my sorrows give a pitying tear;
To each such melting eye, and throbbing heart,
Would gracious Heaven this benefit impart
Never to know my guilt, nor feel my pain:
Then must you own, you ought not to complain;   35
Since you nor weep, nor shall I die, in vain.

[*Exeunt.*]

[Scene XI.

The Place of Execution. The gallows and ladders at the
farther end of the stage. A crowd of spectators.
Blunt and Lucy.

Lucy. Heavens! what a throng!

Blunt. How terrible is death, when thus prepar'd!

Lucy. Support them, Heaven; thou only can
support them; all other help is vain.   5

Officer (within). Make way there; make way,
and give the prisoners room!

Lucy. They are here; observe them well!
How humble and composed young Barnwell
seems! But Millwood looks wild, ruffled with   10
passion, confounded and amazed.

Scene XI. This Scene is not in O1 (1731) or O4 (1732). The
text of this Scene is given from the seventh edition, 1740. In O7
the heading is ‘ Scene the Last.’

Enter Barnwell, Millwood, Officers and Executioners.

Barnwell. See, Millwood, see : our journey's at an end. Life, like a tale that's told, is past away ; that short but dark and unknown passage, death, is all the space 'tween us and endless joys, 15 or woes eternal.

Millwood. Is this the end of all my flattering hopes ? Were youth and beauty given me for a curse, and wisdom only to insure my ruin ? They were, they were ! Heaven, thou hast done thy 20 worst. Or, if thou hast in store some untried plague—somewhat that's worse than shame, despair and death, unpitied death, confirm'd despair and soul confounding shame — something that men and angels can't describe, and only fiends, 25 who bear it, can conceive : now pour it now on this devoted head, that I may feel the worst thou canst inflict, and bid defiance to thy utmost power!

Barn. Yet, ere we pass the dreadful gulph of death — yet, ere you're plunged in everlasting 30 woe : O bend your stubborn knees and harder heart, humbly to deprecate the wrath divine ! Who knows but Heaven, in your dying moments, may bestow that grace and mercy which your life despised ! 33

Mill. Why name you mercy to a wretch like me ? Mercy's beyond my hope—almost beyond my wish. I can't repent, nor ask to be forgiven.

25 *can't.* 1810, cannot.

Barn. O think what 'tis to be for ever, ever miserable; nor with vain pride oppose a Power, that's able to destroy you! 40

Mill. That will destroy me; I feel it will. A deluge of wrath is pouring on my soul. Chains, darkness, wheels, racks, sharp stinging scorpions, molten lead, and seas of sulphur, are light to 45 what I feel.

Barn. O! add not to your vast account despair, a sin more injurious to Heaven than all you've yet committed.

Mill. 'O! I have sin'd beyond the reach of 50 mercy.

Barn. O say not so; 'tis blasphemy to think it. As yon bright roof is higher than the earth, so, and much more, does Heaven's goodness pass our apprehension. O! what created being shall 55 presume to circumscribe mercy, that knows no bounds?

Mill. This yields no hope. Tho' mercy may be boundless, yet 'tis free; and I was doom'd, before the world began, to endless pains, and 60 thou to joys eternal.

Barn. O gracious Heaven! extend thy pity to her! Let thy rich mercy flow in plenteous streams, to chase her fears and heal her wounded soul!

Mill. It will not be. Your prayers are lost 65 in air, or else returned, perhaps with double blessing, to your bosom; but me they help not.

Barn. Yet hear me, Millwood!

Mill. Away, I will not hear thee. I tell thee, youth, I am by Heaven devoted a dreadful in- 70 stance of its power to punish. (*Barnwell seems to pray.*) If thou wilt pray, pray for thyself, not me! How doth his fervent soul mount with his words, and both ascend to Heaven — that Heaven whose gates are shut with adamantine bars 75 against my prayers, had I the will to pray.—I cannot bear it! Sure, 'tis the worst of torments to behold others enjoy that bliss that we must never taste!

Officer. The utmost limit of your time's ex- 80 pired.

Mill. Incompassed with horror, whither must I go? I wou'd not live—nor die. That I cou'd cease to be, or ne'er had been!

Barn. Since peace and comfort are denied 85 her here, may she find mercy where she least expects it, and this be all her hell!—From our example may all be taught to fly the first approach of vice; but, if o'ertaken

By strong temptation, weakness, or surprize, 90
Lament their guilt and by repentance rise!
Th' impenitent alone die unforgiven;
To sin's like man, and to forgive like Heaven.

Exeunt.]

80 *time's.* 1810, time is.
Exeunt. Not in O7; 1810 supplies.

Scene XII.

[Enter] Trueman [to] Blunt and Lucy.

Lucy. Heart-breaking sight ! O wretched, wretched Millwood !

Trueman. You came from her, then ; how is she disposed to meet her fate ?

Blunt. Who can describe unalterable woe ?   5

Lucy. She goes to death encompassed with horror, loathing life, and yet afraid to die ; no tongue can tell her anguish and despair.

True. Heaven be better to her than her fears: may she prove a warning to others, a monument 10 of mercy in her self !

Lucy. O sorrow insupportable ! Break, break, my heart !

True. In vain

With bleeding hearts and weeping eyes we show 15
A humane gen'rous sense of others' woe,
Unless we mark what drew their ruin on,
And, by avoiding that, prevent our own.

Scene XII. In O1 this is Scene XI.   *Enter . . . Lucy.* O7 has only *Enter . . . Trueman,* running this into the preceding scene. Apparently the remaining lines are given as Barnwell and Mildred are led to the gallows.

3 *You came from her, then,* O4 also, evidently placing the scene near the place of execution. O7 omits.

5 *unalterable.* For this 'unutterable' is substituted in the second edition of 1731, and in all the following editions.

FINIS.

EPILOGUE.

Written by COLLEY CIBBER, *Esq.*, and Spoke by
Mrs. CIBBER.

Since fate has robb'd me of the hopeless youth
For whom my heart had hoarded up its truth,
By all the laws of love and honour, now
I'm free again to chuse — and one of you.

   But soft — with caution first I'll round me peep;   5
Maids, in my case, shou'd look before they leap.
Here's choice enough, of various sorts and hue, ⎫
The cit, the wit, the rake cock'd up in cue, ⎬
The fair, spruce mercer, and the tawney Jew. ⎭

   Suppose I search the sober gallery ? — No, ⎫   10
There's none but prentices, and cuckolds all a row ; ⎬
And these, I doubt, are those that make 'em so. ⎭
                  (Pointing to the Boxes.)

   Written by Colley Cibber, Esq. O7 adds : Poet Laureate, and
omits *and spoke by Mrs. Cibber.* The Yale copy of O4 lacks the
last seven lines of the play and the Epilogue, but they probably followed O1.
   Spoke. O7, spoken.   1 *hopeless.* O7, hapless.

'Tis very well, enjoy the jest! But you,
Fine, powder'd sparks—nay, I'm told 'tis true—
Your happy spouses can make cuckolds too.   15
'Twixt you and them, the diff'rence this perhaps,
The cit's asham'd whene'er his duck he traps;
But you, when Madam's tripping, let her fall,
Cock up your hats, and take no shame at all.

What, if some favour'd poet I cou'd meet,   20
Whose love wou'd lay his laurels at my feet?
No; painted passion real love abhors:
His flame wou'd prove the suit of creditors.

Not to detain you, then, with longer pause,
In short, my heart to this conclusion draws: 25
I yield it to the hand that's loudest in applause.

Notes to The London Merchant

Dedication. Sir John Eyles, Baronet. This worthy was a most suitable choice for the dedication of *The London Merchant*. His uncle, John, was Lord Mayor of London in the last year of James II, and was knighted by that sovereign. His father, Francis, was created a baronet by George I, and was an East India Director. Sir John, the second baronet, was a member of the last Parliament of Queen Anne, and of the first and second Parliaments of George I; in the first and second of George II he represented the City of London. In 1727 he was Lord Mayor, and afterwards became Alderman of Bridge-ward Without, 'commonly called Father of the city.' In 1739 he was appointed Postmaster-General. His youngest brother, Joseph, knighted by George I, was likewise an Alderman and a member of the House of Commons. (*The English Baronetage*, vol. IV, 1741.)

3, 1. as Mr. Dryden has some where said. It may be taken as improbable that Dryden anywhere makes use of precisely this expression. But in his *Discourse concerning the Original and Progress of Satire* (1693) he quotes ' our master Aristotle' as saying that ' the most perfect work of Poetry is Tragedy ' ; and he argues in the same sense in the *Essay of Dramatic Poesy*.

3, 7. the end of tragedy. The reference of course is to the Aristotelian theory of the *catharsis*, or purging of the passions, — though it may be doubted whether Lillo understood the nature of the purification of the passions — pity and terror — which Aristotle had in view.

4, 32–33. The strong contrast between a Tamerlane and a Bajazet. Probably Lillo was thinking less of Marlowe's *Tamburlaine the Great*, than of Rowe's *Tamerlane* (1702), in which the contrast in question was intended to illustrate that between William III and Louis XIV.

4, 38–39. The sentiments and examples of a Cato. Addison's *Cato* had been produced in 1713, and still held the stage.

5, 54. in his Hamlet. Act II, Sc. 2.

7, 105-106. at a time when their affairs were in the utmost confusion. This must have been shortly after the bursting of the 'South-Sea Bubble' in 1720.

7, 108-109. attempt your character : attempt to draw a character of you.

Prologue, spoke by Mr. Cibber, Jun. See *Introduction*.

8, 16. In Southern's, Rowe's or Otway's moving strains. See *Introduction*.

9, 26. a thousand-thousand eyes. Cf. *Elmerick*, Act II, *ad fin.* : 'A thousand thousand deaths are in the thought.' See also *The Tempest*, Act III, Sc. 1, *ad fin*.

11, 7. the loan on which he depended from Genoa. See *Introduction*.

12, 35-36. the name of merchant never degrades the gentleman. This was the feeling of Englishmen in the sixteenth and seventeenth centuries, when the younger sons of good houses often went into trade.

15, 19. dispense with my absence. The young lady means : 'dispense with my presence.'

18, 2-3. A little more red. The practice of 'rouging,' though less common in the Elizabethan age than in that of George II, was not unknown to the former. See Hamlet's taunt to Ophelia (*Hamlet*, Act III, Sc. 2) : 'I have heard of your paintings too, well enough'; where Steevens compares the satire on these aids to beauty in Drayton's *Mooncalf*.

19, 30. the Spaniards in the New World. See Prescott's *History of the Conquest of Peru*, bk. IV, chap. 6 : 'Pizarro delivered up the conquered races to his brutal soldiery . . . the towns and villages were given up to pillage ; the wretched natives were parcelled out like slaves, to toil for their conquerors in the mines,' etc.

31, 16-17. while yet in Heaven, bore all his future Hell about him. An apparently original, and a profoundly conceived, refinement upon the thought which in Marlowe's *Doctor Faustus*, Sc. 3, in reply to the question of Faustus :

'How comes it then that you are out of hell ?'

Mephistophilis expresses in the line, of which there are many *analoga* :

'Why this is hell, nor am I out of it.'

35, 91. now must stand on terms: now I must stand on terms.

35, 104–105. the glorious sun . . . once stopp'd his rapid course, and once went back. *Joshua*, x, 13, and *Isaiah*, xxxviii, 8.

35, 108. the sea divided. *Exodus*, xiv, 21.

36, 111–112. men unhurt have walk'd amidst consuming flames. *Daniel*, iii, 25.

36, 112–113. never yet did time, once past, return. This commonplace recalls the ocular demonstration furnished by Friar Bacon's Brazen Head in *Friar Bacon and Friar Bungay*, Sc. xi, that 'Time is,' 'Time was,' and 'Time is past,' are as three tickings of a watch, or three beats of a pulse.

37, 4 (Sc. IV). prevented: anticipated.

65, 15. For him: For he (elliptically).

67, 11. When strong reflections hold the mirror near. The ill-chosen word 'reflections' can here only mean 'thoughts.'

70, 54. The rich man thus, etc. *St. Luke*, xvi, 27–28.

70, 56. The fool, his own soul lost, etc. *St. Luke*, xii, 20.

71, 7. Falsely to accuse ourselves: that we should falsely accuse ourselves.

76, 5. Where shall I hide me? whither shall I fly, etc. Cf. *Psalm* cxxxix, 7 sqq.; and also *Revelation*, vi, 16, and *Hosea*, x, 8. All these passages were possibly in Marlowe's mind when he wrote the first part of Faustus' final speech in *Doctor Faustus*.

79, 2 (Sc. XII). Cannot: canst not. Cf. at the beginning of Sc. xi, Act v (l. 4), of this play : 'Thou only can support them.'

80, 7. this: this is. Several Shakespearean illustrations of this common Elizabethan contraction are cited in Abbott's *Shakespearean Grammar*.

80, 13. Be warn'd, ye youths, etc. This is an expansion of the tag at the end of the old Ballad. See *Appendix A*.

82, 19. credit. In the wider sense of 'honour, reputation.'

88, 35–36. suburb-magistrates. See Sir J. Fitzjames Stephen's *History of the Criminal Law of England*, vol. I (ch. vii), pp. 229–31:

'Throughout a great part of the eighteenth century the business of magistrates in that part of London which was not included in the City was carried on by magistrates who were paid almost entirely by fees. What the fees precisely were, and by what law their exaction was justified, I am not able to say, nor is it worth while to enquire. . . .

'Writing in 1754 (in the Introduction to his *Journal of a Voyage to Lisbon*), Henry Fielding says of his career as a magistrate : " By composing instead of inflaming the quarrels of porters and beggars (which I blush when I say has not been universally practised), and by refusing to take a shilling from a man who most undoubtedly would not have had another left, I reduced an income of about £500 a year of the dirtiest money upon earth to little more than £300, a considerable proportion of which remained with my clerk ; and indeed, if the whole had done so, as it ought, he would be but ill paid for sitting almost sixteen hours in the twenty-four in the most unwholesome as well as nauseous air in the universe, and which has in his case corrupted a good constitution without contaminating his morals."

'He observes in a foot-note : " A predecessor of mine used to boast that he made £1,000 a year in his office, but how he did this (if indeed he did it) is to me a secret." . . .

'. . . Men of genius are exceptions everywhere, but a magistrate ought at least to be, as in these days he is, a gentleman and a man of honour. It was not so in the last century in London. A characteristic account of the " trading justices " was given to the Committee (of the House of Commons) of 1816, by Townsend, a well-known Bow Street runner, who at that time had been in the police thirty-four years or more, *i. e.* since 1782 : " At that time, before the Police Bill took place at all, it was a trading business. . . . The plan used to be to issue out warrants, and take up all the poor devils in the street, and then there was the bailing of them . . . which the magistrates had ; and taking up . . .

girls. . . . They sent none to gaol ; the bailing of them was so much better.''

'These scandals led to the statute, 32 Geo. 3, c. 53, which authorised the establishment of seven public offices in Middlesex and one in Surrey, to each of which three justices were attached. The fees were to be paid by a receiver. . . . The justices were to be paid by a salary of £400 apiece. This experiment proved highly successful.' . . .

As to the generally opprobrious force attaching to the epithet 'suburb,' cf. *infra*, p. 216.

88, 37–38. as the unhospitable natives of Corn-wall do by shipwreck. Cf. *Fatal Curiosity*, Act I (Sc. III, ll. 2–13):

> '. . . savage men, who, more remorseless,
> Prey on shipwreck'd wretches, and spoil and murder those
> Whom fatal tempests and devouring waves,'' etc. . . .

See also *Introduction* to *Fatal Curiosity*.

90, 95. From your destruction raise a nobler name. Gain a higher glory (for their sex) by destroying you (men).

93, 59. learn us : teach us.

95, 41. daily dies. *I Corinthians*, xv, 31.

96, 65. from whence there's no return. Cf. *Hamlet*, Act III, Sc. I :

> 'The undiscover'd country, from whose bourn
> No traveller returns.'

98, 39. We have not yet embrac'd, etc. This answer, says Diderot (*La Lettre de Barnevelt*, — see Introduction), 'is to me of incomparable beauty. . . . I advise anyone who is not deeply affected by these words to let Deucalion or Pyrrha cast him behind them — for he is made of stone.'

102. Trueman and Maria. Diderot comments on this scene as follows (*Entretien sur Le Fils Naturel*): 'Propriety ! Propriety ! I am tired of the word. The woman whom Barnwell loves enters, distracted, into his prison. The two lovers embrace, and fall to the ground.' And he continues that here, as in the agony of Philoctetes, sympathy is assured by absolute truth to nature.

102, 3. reserves: detains. The 'press-yard' in Newgate, with the press-room below for cases which it was deemed necessary to separate from the rest, became a thing of the past soon after the description of it in the *Sketches by Boz* in a paper (*A Visit to Newgate*) of extraordinary graphic power.

103, 29–30. improve the English court, that justly claims such merit. This supplication is hardly less odd if applied to the court of Queen Caroline, than if supposed to refer to that of Queen Elizabeth.

103, 47. condescend to. Descend in order to.

104, 63–64. So the aromatic spices of the East, etc. The simile may possibly have been suggested by *St. John*, XIX, 39.

105, 82. suburb-slaves. It must be remembered that 'suburban respectability' is a conception of modern growth. In the Elizabethan age, and for some time afterwards, the suburbs of London were, like those of fortified towns, regarded as the abode of the lowest classes and the haunts of the dissolute. See Nares, *s. v.*

106, 20–21. Justice and mercy are in Heaven the same. Cf. *The Merchant of Venice*, Act IV, Sc. 1:

> ' — Earthly power doth then show likest God's,
>   When mercy seasons justice.'

109, 44–45. Chains, darkness, wheels, racks, sharp stinging scorpions, etc. Cf. again the final scene in *Doctor Faustus*, and the doomed sinner's cry:

> ' Adders and serpents, let me breathe a while! '

110, 78. Sure, 'tis the worst of torments, etc. ' And in hell he lift up his eyes, being in torments, and seeth Abraham afar off, and Lazarus in his bosom.' *St. Luke*, XVI, 23.

Epilogue. Written by Colley Cibber, Esq., and Spoke by Mrs. Cibber. The first Mrs. Theophilus Cibber was, as has been noted in the *Introduction*, the original representative of Maria.

112, 8. cock'd up in cue: with his hat cocked over his pigtail (*queue*). Mr. Ashton quotes from the *Spectator*, No. 319: 'I observed afterwards that the Variety of Cocks into which he moulded his Hat, not a little contributed to his Impositions upon me.'

112, 9. **the tawney Jew.** 'Tawney' (yellow), as an epithet of derision, referring to the yellow cap or bonnet, the piece of costume obligatory upon Jews. In Barton Booth's acting copy of *The Merchant of Venice*, there is appended to the line—

> 'For sufferance is the badge of all our tribe'—

the stage-direction : 'Showing his yellow cap.'

113, 23. **His flame would prove the suit of creditors** : his passion would prove to be not more disinterested than the suit of a creditor.

Appendix

THE BALLAD OF GEORGE BARNWELL [1]

THE FIRST PART

ALL youths of fair England
  That dwell both far and near,
Regard my story that I tell,
  And to my song give ear.

A London lad I was,
  A merchant's prentice bound ;
My name George Barnwell ; that did spend
  My master many a pound.

Take heed of harlots then,
  And their enticing trains ;
For by that means I have been brought
  To hang alive in chains.

As I upon a day
  Was walking through the street,
About my master's business,
  A wanton I did meet.

[1] Reprinted, slightly re-punctuated, and corrected, from vol. VIII of
English and Scottish Ballads, by F. J. Child, Boston, 1859.

A gallant dainty dame,
    And sumptuous in attire ;
With smiling look she greeted me,
    And did my name require.

Which when I had declar'd,
    She gave me then a kiss,
And said, if I would come to her,
    I should have more than this.

" Fair Mistress," then quoth I,
    " If I the place may know,
This evening I will be with you,
    For I abroad must go,

To gather monies in,
    That are my master's due :
And ere that I do home return,
    I'll come and visit you."

" Good Barnwell," then quoth she,
    " Do thou to Shoreditch come,
And ask for Mistress Millwood's house,
    Next door unto the Gun.[1]

1 Through the kindness of Lieut. Col. W. Evans, who commands the Hon. Artillery Company, I am able to state that the Gun Tavern was in Gun Street, but now fronts into Brushfield Street, a new street running across part of the old Artillery Ground, near Bishopsgate Street Without. The house, which could not have stood on its present site till after the Ground was built over in 1689, is no longer a tavern, and the sign is disused. There is every reason to believe that an older Gun Tavern looked on the Artillery Ground.

And trust me on my truth,
   If thou keep touch with me,
My dearest friend, as my own heart
   Thou shalt right welcome be."

Thus parted we in peace,
   And home I passed right;
Then went abroad, and gather'd in,
   By six o'clock at night,

An hundred pound and one;
   With bag under my arm
I went to Mrs. Millwood's house,
   And thought on little harm.

And, knocking at the door,
   Straightway herself came down;
Rustling in most brave attire,
   With hood and silken gown.

Who, through her beauty bright,
   So gloriously did shine,
That she amaz'd my dazzling eyes.
   She seemèd so divine.

She took me by the hand,
   And, with a modest grace,
" Welcome, sweet Barnwell," then quoth she,
   " Unto this homely place.

And since I have thee found
   As good as thy word to be,
A homely supper, ere we part,
   Thou shalt take here with me."

" O pardon me," quoth I,
   " Fair Mistress, I you pray ;
For why, out of my master's house
   So long I dare not stay."

" Alas, good sir," she said,
   " Are you so strictly ty'd,
You may not with your dearest friend
   One hour or two abide ?

Faith, then the case is hard,
   If it be so," quoth she ;
" I would I were a prentice bound,
   To live along with thee ;

Therefore, my dearest George,
   List well what I shall say,
And do not blame a woman much,
   Her fancy to bewray.[1]

Let not affection's force
   Be counted lewd desire ;
Nor think it not immodesty,
   I should thy love require."

With that she turn'd aside,
   And, with a blushing red,
A mournful motion she bewray'd
   By hanging down her head.

A handkerchief she had,
   All wrought with silk and gold,

[1] Because she betrays her fancy.

Which she, to stay her trickling tears,
  Before her eyes did hold.

This thing unto my sight
  Was wondrous rare and strange,
And in my soul and inward thought
  It wrought a sudden change;

That I so hardy grew
  To take her by the hand,
Saying, " Sweet mistress, why do you
  So dull and pensive stand ?"

" Call me no[t] mistress now,
  But Sarah, thy true friend,
Thy servant, Millwood, honouring thee,
  Until her life hath end.

If thou would'st here alledge
  Thou art in years a boy,
So was Adonis, yet was he
  Fair Venus' only joy."

Thus I, who ne'er before
  Of woman found such grace,
But seeing now so fair a dame
  Give me a kind embrace,

I supt with her that night,
  With joys that did abound;
And for the same paid presently
  In mony twice three pound.

An hundred kisses then
    For my farewel she gave,
Crying, "Sweet Barnwell, when shall I
    Again thy company have?

O stay not hence too long;
    Sweet George, have me in mind";
Her words bewitcht my childishness,
    She utter'd them so kind.

So that I made a vow,
    Next Sunday, without fail,
With my sweet Sarah once again
    To tell some pleasant tale.

When she heard me say so,
    The tears fell from her eye;
"O George," quoth she, "if thou dost fail,
    Thy Sarah sure will dye."

Though long, yet loe! at last,
    The appointed day was come,
That I must with my Sarah meet;
    Having a mighty sum [1]

Of money in my hand,
    Unto her house went I,
Whereas my Love upon her bed
    In saddest sort did lye.

[1] *having a mighty sum.* The having a sum of money with him on Sunday, &c., shows this narrative to have been penned before the Civil Wars: the strict observance of the Sabbath was owing to the change of manners at that period. — PERCY.

" What ails my heart's delight,
    My Sarah dear ? " quoth I ;
" Let not my love lament and grieve,
    Nor sighing pine and die.

But tell me, dearest friend,
    What may thy woes amend,
And thou shalt lack no means of help,
    Though forty pound I spend."

With that she turn'd her head,
    And sickly thus did say :
" Oh me, sweet George, my grief is great ;
    Ten pound I have to pay

Unto a cruel wretch ;
    And God he knows," quoth she,
" I have it not." " Tush, rise," I said,
    " And take it here of me.

Ten pounds, nor ten times ten,
    Shall make my love decay " ;
Then from my bag into her lap
    I cast ten pound straightway.

All blithe and pleasant then,
    To banqueting we go ;
She proffered me to lye with her,
    And said it should be so.

And after that same time
    I gave her store of coyn,
Yea, sometimes fifty pound at once ;
    All which I did purloyn.

And thus I did pass on ;
    Until my master then
Did call to have his reckoning in
    Cast up among his men.

The which when as I heard,
    I knew not what to say ;
For well I knew that I was out
    Two hundred pound that day.

Then from my master straight
    I ran in secret sort ;
And unto Sarah Millwood there
    My case I did report.

But how she us'd this youth,
    In this his care and woe,
And all a strumpet's wiley ways,
    The second part may showe.

THE SECOND PART

"Young Barnwell comes to thee,
    Sweet Sarah, my delight ;
I am undone, unless thou stand
    My faithful friend this night.

Our master to accompts
    Hath just occasion found ;
And I am caught behind the hand
    Above two hundred pound.

And now his wrath to 'scape,
        My love, I fly to thee,
Hoping some time I may remaine
        In safety here with thee."

With that she knit her brows,
        And, looking all aquoy,[1]
Quoth she, " What should I have to do
        With any prentice boy ?

And seeing you have purloyn'd
        Your master's goods away,
The case is bad, and therefore here
        You shall no longer stay."

" My dear, thou know'st," I said,
        " How all which I could get,
I gave it, and did spend it all
        Upon thee every whit."

Quoth she, "Thou art a knave,
        To charge me in this sort,
Being a woman of credit fair,
        And known of good report

Therefore I tell thee flat,
        Be packing with good speed ;

1 *Aquoy*, or acoy. This rare word, of which the latter form occurs in Turberville's *Complaint of the Long Absence of his Love upon First Acquaintance* (Chalmers, II, 640) :

'Why did'st thou show a smiling cheere
        That shouldst have looked *acoy*, — '

and which is connected with the verb *accoy*, to still, calm, *quiet*, appease (see *New English Dictionary*), may here, Professor Skeat thinks, be held to mean ' unconcerned.'

I do defie thee from my heart,
   And scorn thy filthy deed.''

" Is this the friendship that
   You did to me protest ?
Is this the great affection which
   You so to me exprest ?

Now fie on subtle shrews !
   The best is, I may speed
To get a lodging any where
   For money in my need.

False woman, now farewell ;
   Whilst twenty pound doth last,
My anchor in some other haven
   With freedom I will cast.''

When she perceiv'd by this,
   I had store of money there,
" Stay George,'' quoth she, " thou art too quick ;
   Why man, I did but jeer :

Dost think for all my speech,
   That I would let thee go ?
Faith, no,'' said she, " my love to thee
   I-wiss is more than so.''

" You scorne a prentice boy,
   I heard you just now swear ;
Wherefore I will not trouble you '' :
   " Nay, George, hark in thine ear ;

Thou shalt not go to-night,
    What chance soe're befall ;
But, man, we'll have a bed for thee,
    Or else the devil take all.''

So I, by wiles bewitcht
    And snar'd with fancy still,
Had then no power to get [1] away,
    Or to withstand her will.

For wine on wine I call'd,
    And cheer upon good cheer ;
And nothing in the world I thought
    For Sarah's love too dear.

Whilst in her company,
    I had such merriment,
All, all too little I did think,
    That I upon her spent.

" A fig for care and thought !
    When all my gold is gone,
In faith, my girl, we will have more,
    Whoever I light upon.

My father's rich ; why then
    Should I want store of gold ? ''
" Nay, with a father, sure,'' quoth she,
    " A son may well make bold.''

" I've a sister richly wed ;
    I'll rob her ere I'll want.''
" Nay then,'' quoth Sarah, " they may well
    Consider of your scant.''

[1] get. This is Child's emendation for ' put.'

" Nay, I an uncle have ;
 At Ludlow he doth dwell ;
He is a grazier, which in wealth
 Doth all the rest excell.

Ere I will live in lack,
 And have no coyn for thee,
I'll rob his house, and murder him."
 " Why should you not ? " quoth she.

" Was I a man, ere I
 Would live in poor estate,
On father, friends and all my kin,
 I would my talons grate.

For without money, George,
 A man is but a beast ;
But bringing money, thou shalt be
 Always my welcome guest.

For should'st thou be pursued,
 With twenty hues and cryes,
And with a warrant searched for
 With Argus' hundred eyes,

Yet here thou shalt be safe ;
 Such privy wayes there be,
That if they sought an hundred years,
 They could not find out thee."

And so carousing both,
 Their pleasures to content,
George Barnwell had in little space
 His money wholly spent.

Which done, to Ludlow straight
   He did provide to go,
To rob his wealthy uncle there ;
   His minion would it so.

And once he thought to take
   His father by the way,
But that he fear'd his master had
   Took order for his stay. [1]

Unto his uncle then
   He rode with might and main,
Who with a welcome and good cheer
   Did Barnwell entertain.

One fortnight's space he stayed,
   Until it chancèd so,
His uncle with his cattle did
   Unto a market go.

His kinsman rode with him,
   Where he did see right plain,
Great store of money he had took ;
   When, coming home again,

Sudden within a wood,
   He struck his uncle down,
And beat his brains out of his head ;
   So sore he crackt his crown.

Then, seizing fourscore pound,
   To London straight he hyed,

[1] For stopping and apprehending him at his father's. — PERCY.

And unto Sarah Millwood all
The cruell fact descryed.[1]

" Tush, 'tis no matter, George,
So we the money have
To have good cheer in jolly sort,
And deck us fine and brave."

Thus lived in filthy sort,
Until their store was gone :
When means to get them any more,
I-wis poor George had none.

Therefore in railing sort,
She thrust him out of door :
Which is the just reward of those,
Who spend upon a whore.

" O do me not disgrace
In this my need," quoth he ;
She called him thief and murderer,
With all the spight might be.

To the constable she sent,
To have him apprehended ;
And shewed how far, in each degree,
He had the laws offended.

When Barnwell saw her drift,
To sea he got straightway ;
Where fear and sting of conscience
Continually on him lay.

1 *Descryed*, for the rhyme's sake, instead of ' described.'

Unto the lord mayor then,
    He did a letter write;
In which his own and Sarah's fault
    He did at large recite.

Whereby she seizèd was,
    And then to Ludlow sent:
Where she was judg'd, condemn'd and hang'd,
    For murder incontinent.

There dyed this gallant quean,
    Such was her greatest gains;
For murder in Polonia [1]
    Was Barnwell hang'd in chains.

Lo! here's the end of youth
    That after harlots haunt,
Who in the spoil of other men
    About the streets do flaunt.

[1] This is a strange variation of the ordinary termination of the story;
nor was Poland at the time to which the ballad belongs a specially appropriate locality to which to assign the commission of a melodramatic crime.

THE TEXT

The text of *Fatal Curiosity* is printed from the first and only octavo edition, 1737. The British Museum contains a copy of this octavo with MS. annotations, but they are largely arbitrary, sometimes worthless, and may as a group be disregarded. The principles explained as guiding the preparation of *The London Merchant* have been followed with this text. The variants are those of George Colman's revision of 1783, and of the two collective editions of Davies, in 1775 and 1810.

Fatal Curiosity

FATAL CURIOSITY:

A TRUE

TRAGEDY

OF

THREE ACTS.

As it is Acted at the

NEW THEATRE

IN THE

HAY-MARKET.

By Mr. *LILLO*.

LONDON:

Printed for JOHN GRAY at the *Cross-Keys* in the
Poultry near *Cheapside*. MDCCXXXVII.
[Price One Shilling.]

SOURCES

The story on which *Fatal Curiosity* is founded appeared in a black-letter quarto of 1618, entitled *Newes from Perin in Cornwall of a most Bloody and un-exampled Murther very lately committed by a Father on his owne Sonne (who was lately returned from the Indyes) at the Instigation of a mercilesse Step-mother. Together with their Several most wretched endes, being all performed in the Month of September last, Anno 1618.* The story reappeared in W. Sanderson's *Compleat History of the Lives and Reigns of Mary Queen of Scotland, and of her Son and Successor James,* London, 1656, and was reprinted from this book in a folio of 1681 entitled *Annals of the Reigns of King James and King Charles the First. Both of happy memory.* Though published anonymously, the *Annals* are usually known as *Frankland's Annals.* George Colman cites the story from the *Annals* in his *Postscript* to his version of the play, 1782. For the original, Frankland's account, and a list of *analoga,* see *Appendix,* p. 219.

PROLOGUE

Written by HENRY FEILDING, *Esq.;*

Spoken by Mr. ROBERTS

The Tragic Muse has long forgot to please
With Shakespear's *nature,* or with Fletcher's
    ease.
No passion mov'd, thro' five long acts you sit,
Charm'd with the poet's language, or his wit;
Fine things are said, no matter whence they fall: 5
Each single character might speak them all.

  But from this modern fashionable way,
To-night, our author begs your leave to stray.
No fustian hero rages here to-night;
No armies fall, to fix a tyrant's right: 10
From lower life we draw our scene's distress —
Let not your equals move your pity less!
Virtue distrest in humble state support;
Nor think she never lives without the court.

  Tho' to our scenes no royal robes belong,   15
And tho' our little stage as yet be young —
Throw both your scorn and prejudice aside;
Let us with favour, not contempt be try'd;

Thro' the first acts a kind attention lend—
The growing scene shall force you to attend;   20
Shall catch the eyes of every tender fair,
And make them charm their lovers with a tear.
The lover, too, by pity shall impart
His tender passion to his fair one's heart:
The breast which others' anguish cannot move,   25
Was ne'er the seat of friendship, or of love.

[PROLOGUE

Written by GEORGE COLMAN

1782

Spoken by Mr. PALMER

Long since, beneath this humble roof, this play,
Wrought by true *English* genius, saw the day;
Forth from this humble roof it scarce has
    stray'd;
In prouder theatres 'twas never play'd.
There you have gap'd and doz'd o'er many a
    piece   5
Patch'd up from *France*, or stol'n from *Rome*
    or *Greece*,
Or made of shreds from *Shakespear's* golden
    fleece.
There scholars, simple nature cast aside,
Have trick'd their heroes out in classic pride;
No scenes where genuine passion runs to waste, 10
But all hedg'd in by shrubs of modern taste;
Each tragedy laid out like garden grounds:
One circling gravel marks its narrow bounds.
Lillo's plantations were of forest growth,
Shakespear's the same, great Nature's hand in
    both!   15

Give me a tale the passions to controul,
Whose lightest word may harrow up the soul;
A magic potion, of charm'd drugs commixt,
Where pleasure courts, and horror comes be-
    twixt!

Such are the scenes that we this night re-
    new —   20
Scenes that your fathers were well pleas'd to
    view.
Once we half paus'd, and, while cold fears pre-
    vail,
Strove with faint strokes to soften down the
    tale;
But soon, attir'd in all its native woes,
The Shade of LILLO to our fancy rose.   25
' Check thy weak Hand,' it said, or seem'd to
    say,
' Nor of its manly vigour rob my play!
' From British annals I the story drew,
' And British hearts shall feel, and *bear* it too.
' Pity shall move their souls, in spite of rules, 30
' And terror takes no lesson from the schools.
' Speak to their bosoms; to their feelings trust:
' You'll find their sentence *generous* and *just!* ']

DRAMATIS PERSONÆ

MEN

Old *Wilmot*,	Mr. *Roberts.*
Young *Wilmot*,	Mr. *Davies.*
Eustace,	Mr. *Woodburn.*
Randal,	Mr. *Blakes.*

WOMEN

Agnes, wife to Old *Wilmot*,	Mrs. *Charke.*
Charlot,	Miss *Jones.*
Maria,	Miss *Karver.*

Visiters, Men and Women.

SCENE, *Penryn* in *Cornwall.*

𝕱𝖆𝖙𝖆𝖑 𝕮𝖚𝖗𝖎𝖔𝖘𝖎𝖙𝖞

Act I.

Scene 1. *A Room in Wilmot's House.*

Old Wilmot alone.

[*Old Wilmot.*] The day is far advanced; the
    chearful sun
Pursues with vigour his repeated course;
No labour less'ning, nor no time decaying
His strength or splendor. Evermore the same,
From age to age his influence sustains   5
Dependent worlds, bestows both life and motion
On the dull mass that form their dusky orbs,
Chears them with heat, and gilds them with his
    brightness.
Yet man, of jarring elements composed,
Who posts from change to change, from the
    first hour   10
Of his frail being till his dissolution,
Enjoys the sad prerogative above him,
To think, and to be wretched in. What is life
To him that's born to die, or what that wisdom

Whose perfection ends in knowing we know
      nothing!   15
Meer contradiction all — a tragick farce,
Tedious tho' short, and without art elab'rate;
Ridiculously sad —

           Enter Randal.

                Where hast been, Randal?
   Randal. Not out of Penryn, sir; but to the
      strand,
To hear what news from Falmouth since the
      storm   20
Of wind last night.
   O. Wilm.   It was a dreadful one.
   Rand. Some found it so. A noble ship from
      India
Ent'ring in the harbour, run upon a rock,
And there was lost.
   O. Wilm.   What came of those on
      board her?
   Rand. Some few are saved, but much the
      greater part,   25
'Tis thought, are perished.
   O. Wilm.   They are past the fear
Of future tempests, or a wreck on shore;
Those who escaped are still exposed to both.
   Rand. But I've heard news, much stranger
      than this ship-wrack

   29–50 *But I've heard news . . . I understand no riddles.* 1783
omits.

Here in Cornwall. The brave Sir Walter
    Raleigh, 30
Being arrived at Plymouth from Guiana —
A most unhappy voyage — has been betray'd
By base Sir Lewis Stukeley, his own kinsman,
And seiz'd on by an order from the court;
And 'tis reported he must lose his head, 35
To satisfy the Spaniards.
    O. Wilm.   Not unlikely:
His martial genius does not suit the times.
There's now no insolence that Spain can offer
But, to the shame of this pacifick reign,
Poor England must submit to!—Gallant man! 40
Posterity perhaps may do thee justice,
And praise thy courage, learning and integrity,
When thou'rt past hearing; thy successful ene-
    mies,
Much sooner paid, have their reward in hand,
And know for what they labour'd.—Such events 45
Must, questionless, excite all thinking men,
To love and practise virtue!
    Rand.   Nay, 'tis certain,
That virtue ne'er appears so like itself,
So truly bright and great, as when opprest.
    O. Wilm. I understand no riddles.—Where's
    your mistress? 50
    Rand. I saw her pass the High-street t'wards
    the minster.

   O. Wilm. She's gone to visit Charlot. — She
      doth well.
In the soft bosom of that gentle maid
There dwells more goodness than the rigid race
Of moral pedants e'er believ'd or taught.   55
With what amazing constancy and truth
Doth she sustain the absence of our son,
Whom more than life she loves; how shun for
      him,
Whom we shall ne'er see more, the rich and great,
Who own her charms more than supply the want 60
Of shining heaps, and sigh to make her happy!
Since our misfortunes we have found no friend,
None who regarded our distress, but her;
And she, by what I have observed of late,
Is tired, or exhausted — curst condition,   65
To live a burden to one only friend,
And blast her youth with our contagious woe!
Who that had reason, soul, or sense, would
      bear it
A moment longer! — [*Aside.*] Then, this hon-
      est wretch! —
I must dismiss him; why should I detain,   70
A grateful, gen'rous youth to perish with me?
His service may procure him bread elsewhere,
Tho' I have none to give him. — Prithee, Ran-
      dal!
How long hast thou been with me?

 Rand.   Fifteen years.
I was a very child, when first you took me, 75
To wait upon your son, my dear young master.
I oft have wish'd I'd gone to India with him;
Tho' you, desponding, give him o'er for lost.
       Old Wilmot wipes his eyes.
I am to blame — this talk revives your sorrow
For his absence.
 O. Wilm.   How can that be reviv'd 80
Which never died?
 Rand.   The whole of my intent
Was to confess your bounty, that supplied
The loss of both my parents; I was long
The object of your charitable care.
 O. Wilm. No more of that! Thou'st served
    me longer since 85
Without reward; so that account is balanced,
Or rather I'm thy debtor: I remember —
When poverty began to show her face
Within these walls, and all my other servants,
Like pamper'd vermin from a falling house, 90
Retreated with the plunder they had gain'd,
And left me, too indulgent and remiss
For such ungrateful wretches to be crush'd
Beneath the ruin they had helped to make —
That you, more good than wise, refused to
    leave me. 95

  80 *How can that.* 1783, That cannot.

Rand. Nay, I beseech you, sir!

 O. Wilm.   With my distress,
In perfect contradiction to the world,
Thy love, respect, and diligence increased.
Now, all the recompence within my power
Is to discharge thee, Randal, from my hard, 100
Unprofitable service.

 Rand.   Heaven forbid!
Shall I forsake you in your worst necessity?
Believe me, sir, my honest soul abhors
The barb'rous thought.

 O. Wilm.   What! can'st thou feed on air?
I have not left wherewith to purchase food 105
For one meal more.

 Rand.   Rather than leave you thus,
I'll beg my bread and live on others bounty,
While I serve you.

 O. Wilm. [*aside*].   Down, down my swell-
   ing heart,
Or burst in silence! 'Tis thy cruel fate
Insults thee by his kindness. He is innocent 110
Of all the pain it gives thee. — Go thy ways!
I will no more suppress thy youthful hopes
Of rising in the world.

 Rand.   'Tis true; I'm young,
And never tried my fortune, or my genius,
Which may perhaps find out some happy means, 115
As yet unthought of, to supply your wants.

O. Wilm. Thou tortur'st me : I hate all ob-
    ligations
Which I can ne'er return — and who art thou,
That I shou'd stoop to take 'em from thy hand?
Care for thy self, but take no thought for me ! 120
I will not want thee; trouble me no more !
   Rand. Be not offended, sir, and I will go.
I ne'er repined at your commands before ;
But, heaven's my witness, I obey you now
With strong reluctance and a heavy heart. 125
Farewel, my worthy master !   *Going.*
   O. Wilm.   Farewel — stay !
As thou art yet a stranger to the world,
Of which, alas ! I've had too much experi-
    ence,
I shou'd, methinks, before we part, bestow
A little counsel on thee. Dry thy eyes.— 130
If thou weep'st thus, I shall proceed no far-
    ther.
Dost thou aspire to greatness or to wealth,
Quit books and the unprofitable search
Of wisdom there, and study human-kind !
No science will avail thee without that ; 135
But, that obtain'd, thou need'st not any other.
This will instruct thee to conceal thy views,
And wear the face of probity and honour,
'Till thou hast gain'd thy end, which must be
    ever

Thy own advantage, at that man's expense   140
Who shall be weak enough to think thee hon-
      est.

   Rand. You mock me, sure!

   O. Wilm.   I never was more serious.

   Rand. Why should you counsel what you
      scorned to practise?

   O. Wilm. Because that foolish scorn has been
      my ruin.

I've been an idiot, but would have thee wiser,   145
And treat mankind as they would treat thee,
      Randal —
As they deserve, and I've been treated by 'em.
Thou'st seen by me and those who now despise
      me,
How men of fortune fall and beggars rise:
Shun my example, treasure up my precepts;   150
The world's before thee — be a knave and pros-
      per! —

(*After a long pause.*) What, art thou dumb?

   Rand.   Amazement ties my tongue.
Where are your former principles?

   O. Wilm.   No matter;
Suppose I have renounced 'em! I have pas-
      sions,
And love thee still; therefore would have thee
      think,   155
The world is all a scene of deep deceit,

And he who deals with mankind on the square
Is his own bubble, and undoes himself.   *Exit.*
   Rand. Is this the man I thought so wise and
      just?
What, teach and counsel me to be a villain!   160
Sure, grief has made him frantick, or some fiend
Assum'd his shape — I shall suspect my senses!
High-minded he was ever, and improvident,
But pitiful and generous to a fault:
Pleasure he loved, but honour was his idol.   165
O fatal change! O horrid transformation!
So a majestic temple sunk to ruin,
Becomes the loathsome shelter and abode
Of lurking serpents, toads, and beasts of prey;
And scaly dragons hiss, and lions roar,   170
Where wisdom taught and musick charm'd be-
      fore.   *Exit.*

Scene II.

A Parlour in Charlot's House.

Enter Charlot and Maria.

   Charlot. What terror and amazement must
     they feel
Who die by ship-wrack!
   Maria.   'Tis a dreadful thought!

158 *undoes himself.* 1783 adds:
      Farewell, and mark my counsel, boy!
        Rand.   Amazement!

Char. Ay ; is it not, Maria ? To descend,
Living and conscious, to that watry tomb !
Alas ! had we no sorrows of our own,   5
The frequent instances of others woe
Must give a gen'rous mind a world of pain.
But, you forget, you promised me to sing.
Tho' chearfulness and I have long been strang-
       ers,
Harmonious sounds are still delightful to me.   10
There is in melody a secret charm
That flatters, while it adds to, my disquiet,
And makes the deepest sadness the most pleasing.
There's, sure, no passion in the human soul
But finds its food in musick. — I wou'd hear   15
The song composed by that unhappy maid,
Whose faithful lover scaped a thousand perils
From rocks, and sands, and the devouring deep,
And, after all, being arrived at home,
Passing a narrow brook, was drownèd there,   20
And perished in her sight.

SONG.

Mar.   *Cease, cease, heart-easing tears ;*
       Adieu, you flatt'ring fears,
       Which seven long tedious years
         Taught me to bear !   25
       Tears are for lighter woes ;
       Fear no such danger knows,
       As fate remorseless shows—
         Endless despair.

11–13 *There is in melody . . . most pleasing.* 1783 omits.

> *Dear cause of all my pain,*　　　　　　30
> *On the wide, stormy main*
> *Thou wast preserved in vain,*
> 　*Tho' still adored;*
> *Had'st thou died there, unseen,*
> *My blasted eyes had been*　　　　　　35
> *Saved from the horrid'st scene*
> 　*Maid e'er deplored!*

　　　　　　　　　　Charlot finds a letter.

Char. What's this? — A letter superscribed
　　to me?
None could convey it here but you, Maria.
Ungen'rous, cruel maid, to use me thus;　　40
To join with flatt'ring men to break my peace,
And persecute me to the last retreat!
　　Mar. Why should it break your peace to hear
　　　　the sighs
Of honourable love, and know th' effects
Of your resistless charms? This letter is —　　45
　　Char. No matter whence — return it back
　　　　unopen'd!
I have no love, no charms but for my Wilmot,
Nor would have any.
　　Mar.　　　　　　Strange infatuation!
Why should you waste the flower of your days
In fruitless expectation? Wilmot's dead —　　50
Or, living, dead to you.

　　48–50 *Strange infatuation . . . fruitless expectation.* 1783
omits; adding after *would have any:* 'Alas!'

Char.   I'll not despair.
Patience shall cherish hope, nor wrong his
        honour
By unjust suspicion. I know his truth,
And will preserve my own. But, to prevent
All future vain, officious importunity,   55
Know, thou incessant foe of my repose:
Whether he sleeps, secure from mortal cares,
In the deep bosom of the boist'rous main,
Or, tost with tempests, still endures its rage;
Whether his weary pilgrimage by land   60
Has found an end, and he now rests in peace
In earth's cold womb, or wanders o'er her face;
Be it my lot to waste in pining grief
The remnant of my days for his known loss,
Or live, as now, uncertain and in doubt —   65
No second choice shall violate my vows.
High heaven, which heard them, and abhors
        the perjured,
Can witness, they were made without reserve,
Never to be retracted, ne'er dissolved
By accidents or absence, time or death.   70
    Mar. I know, and long have known, my
        honest zeal

58–65 *In the deep bosom . . . and in doubt.* 1783 omits.
    71–73 *I know, and long . . . for flatt'ry.* 1783 omits, and
reads the ensuing passage as follows :

        And did your vows oblige you to support
        His haughty parents, to your utter ruin,
        Well may you weep to think on what you've done.

To serve you gives offence. But be offended:
This is no time for flatt'ry. Did your vows
Oblige you to support his gloomy, proud,
Impatient parents, to your utter ruin,   75
You well may weep to think on what you've
            done.

 Char. I weep to think that I can do no more
For their support. What will become of 'em,
The hoary, helpless, miserable pair!

 Mar. Then all these tears, this sorrow is for
            them?   80

 Char. Taught by afflictions, I have learn'd to
            bear
Much greater ills than poverty with patience.
When luxury and ostentation's banish'd,
The calls of nature are but few; and those
These hands, not used to labour, may supply.   85
But when I think on what my friends must suffer,
My spirits fail, and I'm o'erwhelm'd with grief.

 Mar. What I wou'd blame you force me to
            admire,
And mourn for you, as you lament for them.
Your patience, constancy, and resignation   90
Merit a better fate.

 Char.   So pride would tell me,

---

76 *You well may.* 1783, Well may you.
80–87 *Then all these tears . . . with grief.* 1783 omits.
88 *I wou'd blame.* 1783, I can't praise.

And vain self-love; but I believe them not;
And, if by wanting pleasure I have gained
Humility, I'm richer for my loss.

    Mar. You have the heavenly art, still to
      improve   95
Your mind by all events.——But here comes one,
Whose pride seems to increase with her mis-
    fortunes.

                Enter Agnes.

Her faded dress, unfashionably fine,
As ill conceals her poverty as that
Strain'd complaisance her haughty, swelling
    heart.   100
Tho' perishing with want, so far from asking,
She ne'er receives a favour unconpelled,
And, while she ruins, scorns to be obliged.
She wants me gone, and I abhor her sight.

                        Ex[*it*] *Mar*[*ia*].

    Char. This visit's kind.

    Agnes.   Few else would think it so. 105
Those who would once have thought them-
    selves much honoured
By the least favour, tho' 'twere but a look,
I could have shown them, now refuse to see me.

    104 *She wants me gone, and I abhor her sight.* 1783 reads,
instead of this line: Let me depart, I know she loves me not.
In 1783 *Enter Agnes* is placed after *Exit Maria*; instead of before
Her faded. In 1810 the stage-direction after *I abhor her sight* is:
[*Aside. Exit.*

'Tis misery enough to be reduced
To the low level of the common herd,   110
Who, born to begg'ry, envy all above them;
But 'tis the curse of curses to endure
The insolent contempt of those we scorn.

   Char. By scorning, we provoke them to con-
      tempt,
And thus offend, and suffer in our turns.   115
We must have patience.

   Agn.   No, I scorn them yet.
But there's no end of suff'ring; who can say
Their sorrows are compleat? My wretched hus-
      band,
Tired with our woes and hopeless of relief,
Grows sick of life —

   Char.   May gracious Heaven support him! 120

   Agn. And, urged by indignation and despair,
Would plunge into eternity at once
By foul self-murder. His fixed love for me,
Whom he would fain persuade to share his fate,
And take the same, uncertain, dreadful course, 125
Alone withholds his hand —

   Char.   And may it ever!

   Agn. I've known with him the two extremes
      of life,

   120 *May . . . him. Agn.* 1783 omits.
   123 *By foul self-murder.* 1783 inserts between this and *His
fixed: Char.* Gracious Heav'n support him.

The highest happiness and deepest woe,
With all the sharp and bitter aggravations
Of such a vast transition. Such a fall   130
In the decline of life! I have as quick,
As exquisite a sense of pain as he,
And wou'd do any thing but die, to end it —
But there my courage fails. Death is the worst
That fate can bring, and cuts off ev'ry hope.   135
    Char. We must not chuse, but strive to bear
        our lot
Without reproach or guilt. But by one act
Of desperation, we may overthrow
The merit we've been raising all our days;
And lose our whole reward. And now, me-
        thinks,   140
Now more than ever, we have cause to fear,
And be upon our guard. The hand of Heaven
Spreads clouds on clouds o'er our benighted
        heads,
And, wrapt in darkness, doubles our distress.
I had, the night last past, repeated twice,   145
A strange and awful dream. I would not yield
To fearful superstition, nor despise
The admonition of a friendly power
That wished my good.

   137 *one act.* 1783, one rash act.
   142–144 *The hand of Heaven . . . doubles our distress.* 1783
omits.

   Agn.   I've certain plagues enough,
Without the help of dreams, to make me
     wretched.   150
   Char. I wou'd not stake my happiness or
     duty
On their uncertain credit, nor on aught
But reason, and the known decrees of Heaven.
Yet dreams have sometimes shewn events to
     come,
And may excite to vigilance and care,   155
In some important hour, when all our weakness
Shall be attacked, and all our strength be need-
     ful,
To shun the gulph that gapes for our destruction,
And fly from guilt and everlasting ruin.
My vision may be such, and sent to warn us,   160
Now we are tried by multiplied afflictions,
To mark each motion of our swelling hearts,
And not attempt to extricate ourselves,
And seek deliverance by forbidden ways;
But keep our hopes and innocence entire,   165
'Till we're dismist, to join the happy dead
In that bless'd world, where transitory pain,
And frail, imperfect virtue, is rewarded
With endless pleasure and consummate joy—
Or heaven relieves us here.

   156–159 *In some important . . . everlasting ruin.* 1783 omits.
   165 *But keep.* 1783, To keep.
   167–170 *In that bless'd . . . relieves us here.* 1783 omits.

　　Agn.　　　　　　　　　　Well; pray, proceed! 170
You've rais'd my curiosity at least.
　　Char. Methought, I sate, in a dark winter's
　　　　night,
My garments thin, my head and bosom bare,
On the wide summit of a barren mountain,
Defenceless and exposed, in that high region,　175
To all the cruel rigors of the season.
The sharp bleak winds pierced thro' my shiv'r-
　　　　ing frame,
And storms of hail, and sleet, and driving rains
Beat with impetuous fury on my head,
Drench'd my chill'd limbs, and pour'd a deluge
　　　　round me.　　　　　　　　　　　180
On one hand, ever gentle patience sate,
On whose calm bosom I reclin'd my head,
And on the other, silent contemplation.
At length, to my unclosed and watchful eyes,
That long had roll'd in darkness, and oft raised 185
Their chearless orbs towards the starless sky,
And sought for light in vain, the dawn ap-
　　　　peared;
And I beheld a man, an utter stranger,
But of a graceful and exalted mein,

　　170 *pray, proceed!* For this 1783 reads: To your dream!
　　171 *You've rais'd . . . at least.* 1783 omits.
　　173 *My garments . . . bosom bare.* 1783 omits.
　　175–176 *Defenceless . . . season.* 1783 omits.
　　185–187 *and oft raised . . . in vain, the.* 1783 omits.

Who press'd with eager transport to embrace me. 190
— I shunn'd his arms; but, at some words he
    spoke,
Which I have now forgot, I turn'd again;
But he was gone; and — oh, transporting
    sight! —
Your son, my dearest Wilmot, fill'd his place.
  Agn. If I regarded dreams, I should expect 195
Some fair event from yours; I have heard no-
    thing
That should alarm you yet.
  Char.   But what's to come,
Tho' more obscure, is terrible indeed.
Methought, we parted soon, and, when I sought
    him,
You and his father—yes, you both were there— 200
Strove to conceal him from me; I pursued
You with my cries, and call'd on Heaven and
    earth
To judge my wrongs, and force you to reveal
Where you had hid my love, my life, my Wil-
    mot! —
  Agn. Unless you mean t'affront me, spare
    the rest!   205
'Tis just as likely Wilmot should return,
As we become your foes.

196–197 *I have heard . . . you yet.* 1783 omits.
202 *You with my cries.* 1783 inserts 'both' after *You*.

Char. Far be such rudeness
From Charlot's thoughts! But, when I heard
you name
"Self-murder," it reviv'd the frightful image
Of such a dreadful scene.

Agn. You will persist!——210

Char. Excuse me; I have done. Being a
dream,
I thought, indeed, it cou'd not give offence.

Agn. Not, when the matter of it is offen-
sive!——
You cou'd not think so, had you thought at all;
But I take nothing ill from thee—adieu; 215
I've tarried longer than I first intended,
And my poor husband mourns the while alone.

Exit Agnes.

Char. She's gone abruptly, and, I fear, dis-
pleas'd.
The least appearance of advice or caution
Sets her impatient temper in a flame. 220
When grief, that well might humble, swells our
pride,
And pride increasing, aggravates our grief,
The tempest must prevail 'till we are lost.

---

208 *From Charlot's thoughts!* 1783, From Charlot's breast!
209–210 *the frightful image Of such a dreadful scene.* 1737
and 1810 run this into one line.
213 *Not, when.* The editions interpunctuate *Not when.*

When Heaven, incensed, proclaims unequal
  war
With guilty earth, and sends its shafts from
  far,   225
No bolt descends to strike, no flame to burn
The humble shrubs that in low valleys
  mourn ;
While mountain pines, whose lofty heads as-
  pire
To fan the storm, and wave in fields of fire,
And stubborn oaks that yield not to its force, 230
Are burnt, o'erthrown, or shiver'd in its
  course.

Scene III.

The Town and Port of Penryn.

Enter Young Wilmot and Eustace in Indian habits.

Young Wilmot. Welcome, my friend, to Penryn ; here we're safe.
Eustace. Then, we're deliver'd twice : first
  from the sea,
And then from savage men, who, more remorseless,

---

224 *When Heaven, etc.* The remainder of this speech, given
in 1775 and 1810, is omitted in 1783 ; but after *'till we are lost*,
the line is there added :

   Heaven grant a fairer issue to her sorrows !

Prey on shipwreck'd wretches, and spoil and
      murder those
Whom fatal tempests and devouring waves,   5
In all their fury spar'd.
    Y. Wilm.   It is a scandal,
Tho' malice must acquit the better sort,
The rude unpolisht people here in Cornwall
Have long laid under, and with too much jus-
      tice.
Cou'd our superiors find some happy means   10
To mend it, they would gain immortal honour;
For 'tis an evil grown almost invet'rate,
And asks a bold and skilful hand to cure.
    Eust. Your treasure's safe, I hope.
    Y. Wilm.   'Tis here, thank Heaven!
Being in jewels, when I saw our danger,   15
I hid it in my bosom.
    Eust.   I observed you,
And wonder how you could command your
      thoughts,
In such a time of terror and confusion.
    Y. Wilm. My thoughts were then at home—
      O England! England!
Thou seat of plenty, liberty and health,   20
With transport I behold thy verdant fields,

5 *fatal.* 1783, fell.
10-11 *Cou'd our . . . honour.* 1783 omits.
12 *invet'rate.* 1737, inv'terate.

Thy lofty mountains rich with useful ore,
Thy numerous herds, thy flocks, and winding
  streams!
After a long and tedious absence, Eustace,
With what delight we breathe our native air, 25
And tread the genial soil that bore us first!
'Tis said, the world is ev'ry wise man's country;
Yet, after having view'd its various nations,
I'm weak enough still to prefer my own
To all I've seen beside. You smile, my friend, 30
And think, perhaps, 'tis instinct more than rea-
  son?
Why, be it so! Instinct preceded reason
In the wisest of us all, and may sometimes
Be much the better guide. But, be it either,
I must confess that even death itself 35
Appeared to me with twice its native horrors,
When apprehended in a foreign land.
Death is, no doubt, in ev'ry place the same;
Yet observation must convince us, most men,
Who have it in their power, chuse to expire 40
Where they first drew their breath.
  Eust.   Believe me, Wilmot!
Your grave reflections were not what I smil'd at;
I own their truth. That we're return'd to Eng-
  land

33 *In the wisest of us all.* 1783, Ev'n in the wisest men.
39 *Yet observation must convince us, most men.* 1783, Yet
nature casts a look towards home, and most.

Affords me all the pleasure you can feel
Merely on that account; yet I must think 45
A warmer passion gives you all this transport.
You have not wander'd, anxious and impatient,
From clime to clime, and compast sea and land
To purchase wealth, only to spend your days
In idle pomp and luxury at home. 50
I know thee better: thou art brave and wise,
And must have nobler aims.

  Y. Wilm.   O Eustace! Eustace!
Thou knowest, for I've confest to thee, I love;
But, having never seen the charming maid,
Thou canst not know the fierceness of my flame. 55
My hopes and fears, like the tempestuous seas
That we have past, now mount me to the skies,
Now hurl me down from that stupendous height,
And drive me to the center. Did you know
How much depends on this inportant hour, 60
You wou'd not be surprized to see me thus.
The sinking fortune of our ancient house,
Which time and various accidents had wasted,
Compelled me young to leave my native country,
My weeping parents, and my lovely Charlot, 65
Who ruled, and must for ever rule my fate.

45 *yet I must think.* 1783 begins a line with these words, and
continues: a warmer passion moves you; Thinking of that I
smiled.

45-52 *Merely on that . . . nobler aims.* 1783 omits.

53 *knowest,* 1737, 1775. 1783, 1810, know'st.

How I've improv'd, by care and honest com-
    merce,
My little stock, you are in part a witness.
'Tis now seven tedious years, since I set forth:
And as th'uncertain course of my affairs   70
Bore me from place to place, I quickly lost
The means of corresponding with my friends.
——O! shou'd my Charlot, doubtful of my
    truth,
Or in despair ever to see me more,
Have given herself to some more happy lover—— 75
Distraction's in the thought!—or shou'd my
    parents,
Grieved for my absence and opprest with want,
Have sunk beneath their burden, and expired,
While I too late was flying to relieve them:
The end of all my long and weary travels,   80
The hope, that made success itself a blessing,
Being defeated and for ever lost,
What were the riches of the world to me?

    Eust. The wretch who fears all that is possible,
Must suffer more than he who feels the worst 85
A man can feel who lives exempt from fear.
A woman may be false, and friends are mortal;
And yet, your aged parents may be living,
And your fair mistress constant.

    67–72 *How I've improved . . . with my friends.* 1783
omits.

Y. Wilm.   True, they may ;
I doubt, but I despair not. No, my friend !   90
My hopes are strong and lively as my fears,
And give me such a prospect of my happiness
As nothing but fruition can exceed.
They tell me, Charlot is as true as fair,
As good as wise, as passionate as chaste ;   95
That she with fierce impatience, like my own,
Laments our long and painful separation ;
That we shall meet, never to part again ;
That I shall see my parents, kiss the tears
From their pale hollow cheeks, chear their sad
        hearts,   100
And drive that gaping phantom, meagre want,
For ever from their board ; crown all their days
To come with peace, with pleasure and abund-
        ance ;
Receive their fond embraces and their blessings,
And be a blessing to 'em.

Eust.   'Tis our weakness : 105
Blind to events, we reason in the dark,
And fondly apprehend what none e'er found,
Or ever shall — pleasure and pain unmixt ;
And flatter and torment ourselves by turns,
With what shall never be.

     92–93 *And give me such . . . can exceed.* 1783 omits.
     95–97 *As good as wise . . . separation.* 1783 omits.
     102–103 *crown all their days To come.* 1783, their days to come
Crown all.

Y. Wilm.   I'll go this instant   110
To seek my Charlot, and explore my fate.

Eust. What, in that foreign habit?

Y. Wilm.   That's a trifle,
Not worth my thoughts.

Eust.   The hardships you've endured,
And your long stay beneath the burning zone,
Where one eternal sultry summer reigns,   115
Have marr'd the native hue of your complexion.
Methinks, you look more like a sun-burnt Indian,
Than a Briton.

Y. Wilm.   Well, 'tis no matter, Eustace!
I hope my mind's not alter'd for the worse;
And, for my outside — but inform me, friend,   120
When I may hope to see you?

Eust.   When you please;
You'll find me at the inn.

Y. Wilm. When I have learnt my doom,
          expect me there!
'Till then, farewel!

Eust. Farewel! Success attend you!   125
                    Ex[it] Eustace.

Y. Wilm. "We flatter, and torment our-
          selves, by turns,
" With what shall never be." Amazing folly!
We stand exposed to many unavoidable

125 *Success attend you!* 1783 after this has the stage-direction:
Exeunt severally.

Calamities, and therefore fondly labour
T'increase their number, and inforce their
      weight,   130
By our fantastic hopes and groundless fears.
  For one severe distress imposed by fate,

  What numbers doth tormenting fear create!
  Deceiv'd by hope, Ixion-like, we prove
  Immortal joys, and seem to rival Jove;   135
  The cloud dissolv'd, impatient we complain,
  And pay for fancied bliss substantial pain.
                         [*Exit.*]

      132–137 *For . . . pain.* 1783 omits.

Act II.

Scene I. *Charlot's House.*

Enter Charlot, thoughtful; and soon after Maria
from the other side.

Maria. Madam, a stranger in a foreign habit
Desires to see you.

    Charlot.   In a foreign habit?
'Tis strange, and unexpected — but admit him.

                  Exit Maria.
Who can this stranger be? I know no foreigner,

        Enter Young Wilmot.
— Nor any man like this.

    Y. Wilmot.   Ten thousand joys! 5

              Going to embrace her.

    Char. You are rude, sir — pray, forbear, and
    let me know
What business brought you here, or leave the
    place!

    Y. Wilm. (aside). She knows me not, or will
    not seem to know me.
Perfidious maid! Am I forgot or scorned?

    Char. Strange questions from a man I never
    knew!   10

---

1 *Maria.* 1783, Serv.   6 *pray, forbear.* 1783, forbear.
8 *aside.* 1783 omits the direction.

Y. Wilm. (*aside*). With what aversion and
  contempt she views me!
My fears are true; some other has her heart;
She's lost; my fatal absence has undone me. —
Oh, cou'd thy Wilmot have forgot thee, Char-
  lot?
 Char. Ha! "Wilmot!" Say, what do your
  words import?   15
O gentle stranger, ease my swelling heart,
That else will burst! Canst thou inform me
  ought?
What dost thou know of Wilmot?
 Y. Wilm.   This I know,
When all the winds of heaven seem'd to con-
  spire
Against the stormy main, and dreadful peals 20
Of rattling thunder deafen'd ev'ry ear,
And drown'd th'affrighten'd mariners loud cries;
While livid lightning spread its sulphurous flames
Thro' all the dark horizon, and disclos'd
The raging seas incensed to his destruction; 25
When the good ship in which he was embark'd,
Unable longer to support the tempest,
Broke and, o'erwhelm'd by the impetuous surge,
Sunk to the oozy bottom of the deep,
And left him struggling with the warring waves:— 30

  17 *Canst thou inform me ought?* 1783 omits.
  27 *Unable . . . tempest.* 1783 omits.

In that dread moment, in the jaws of death,
When his strength fail'd and ev'ry hope forsook
      him,
And his last breath press'd t'wards his trembling
      lips,
The neighbouring rocks, that echoed to his
      moan,
Returned no sound articulate but " Charlot ! "   35
  Char. The fatal tempest, whose description
    strikes
The hearer with astonishment, is ceased ;
And Wilmot is at rest. The fiercer storm
Of swelling passions, that o'erwhelms the soul
And rages worse than the mad foaming seas   40
In which he perish'd, ne'er shall vex him more.
  Y. Wilm. Thou seem'st to think, he's dead.
    Enjoy that thought;
Persuade yourself that what you wish is true,
And triumph in your falshood ! Yes, he's dead ;
You were his fate. The cruel winds and waves,   45
That cast him pale and breathless on the shore,
Spared him for greater woes : to know, his Char-
    lot,
Forgetting all her vows to him and Heaven,
Had cast him from her thoughts. Then, then
    he died ;
But never must have rest. Ev'n now he wanders,   50

   50 *But never must have rest*. 1783, But never can have rest.

A sad, repining, discontented ghost,
The unsubstantial shadow of himself,
And pours his plaintive groans in thy deaf ears,
And stalks, unseen, before thee.

    Char.   'Tis enough!
Detested falshood now has done its worst. ——   55
And art thou dead, and wou'd'st thou die, my
       Wilmot,
For one thou thought'st unjust, thou soul of
      truth !
What must be done ? Which way shall I ex-
      press
Unutterable woe, or how convince
Thy dear departed spirit of the love,   60
Th'eternal love and never-failing faith
Of thy much injur'd, lost, despairing Charlot ?

    Y. Wilm. (*aside*). Be still, my flutt'ring heart;
        hope not too soon !
Perhaps I dream, and this is all illusion.

    Char. If, as some teach, the mind intuitive,   65
Free from the narrow bounds and slavish ties
Of sordid earth, that circumscribe its power
While it remains below, roving at large,

---

    56 *And art thou dead, and wou'd'st.* The editions interpunc-
tuate, *And art thou dead ? And wou'd'st.*

    57 *unjust, thou.* The editions interpunctuate, *unjust ? Thou.*

    66 *Free from . . . ties.* 1783, Free from the bounds and ties
of sordid earth.

    67 *Of sordid earth, that circumscribe its power.* 1783 omits.

    68 *While . . . large.* 1783 omits.

Can trace us to our most concealed retreat,
See all we act, and read our very thoughts :   70
To thee, O Wilmot, kneeling I appeal :
If e'er I swerv'd in action, word, or thought
From the severest constancy and truth,
Or ever wish'd to taste a joy on earth
That center'd not in thee, since last we part-
    ed :   75
May we ne'er meet again, but thy loud wrongs
So close the ear of mercy to my cries,
That I may never see those bright abodes
Where truth and virtue only have admission,
And thou inhabit'st now !
   Y. Wilm.   Assist me, Heaven ! 80
Preserve my reason, memory and sense !
O moderate my fierce tumultuous joys,
Or their excess will drive me to distraction !
O Charlot ! Charlot ! lovely, virtuous maid !
Can thy firm mind, in spite of time and ab-
    sence,   85
Remain unshaken, and support its truth,
And yet thy frailer memory retain
No image, no idea of thy lover ?
Why dost thou gaze so wildly ?   Look on me ;
Turn thy dear eyes this way ; observe me well ! 90
Have scorching climates, time, and this strange
    habit

    73 *From the . . . and truth.* 1783 omits.

So changed and so disguised thy faithful Wilmot,
That nothing in my voice, my face, or mien,
Remains to tell my Charlot I am he?

> *After viewing him some time, she approaches*
> *weeping, and gives him her hand; and*
> *then, turning towards him, sinks upon his*
> *bosom.*

Why dost thou weep? Why dost thou tremble
  thus?   95
Why doth thy panting heart and cautious touch
Speak thee but half convinc'd? Whence are thy
  fears?
Why art thou silent? Canst thou doubt me
  still?
 Char. No, Wilmot, no! I'm blind with too
  much light.
O'ercome with wonder, and opprest with joy; 100
The struggling passions barr'd the doors of
  speech,
But speech, enlarg'd, affords me no relief.
This vast profusion of extream delight,
Rising at once and bursting from despair,
Defies the aid of words, and mocks description. 105
But for one sorrow, one sad scene of anguish,
That checks the swelling torrent of my joys,
I could not bear the transport.
 Y. Wilm.   Let me know it;

101–102 *The struggling passions . . . relief.* 1783 omits.

Give me my portion of thy sorrow, Charlot!
Let me partake thy grief, or bear it for thee!   110
   Char. Alas, my Wilmot! These sad tears are
     thine;
They flow for thy misfortunes. I am pierced
With all the agonies of strong compassion,
With all the bitter anguish you must feel,
When you shall hear, your parents —
   Y. Wilm.   Are no more!   115
   Char. You apprehend me wrong.
   Y. Wilm.   Perhaps I do;
Perhaps you mean to say, the greedy grave
Was satisfied with one, and one is left
To bless my longing eyes? But which, my
     Charlot?
—And yet, forbear to speak, 'till I have thought—   120
   Char. Nay, hear me, Wilmot!
   Y. Wilm.   I perforce must hear thee.
For I might think 'till death, and not deter-
     mine,
Of two so dear which I could bear to lose.
   Char. Afflict yourself no more with ground-
     less fears:
Your parents both are living. Their distress,   125
The poverty to which they are reduced,
In spight of my weak aid, was what I mourned;
And that in helpless age, to them whose youth

120–123 *And yet, forbear . . . bear to lose.* 1783 omits.

Was crown'd with full prosperity, I fear,
Is worse, much worse, than death.
    Y. Wilm.   My joy's compleat! 130
My parents living, and possess'd of thee ! —
From this blest hour, the happiest of my life,
I'll date my rest. My anxious hopes and fears,
My weary travels, and my dangers past,
Are now rewarded all; now I rejoice   135
In my success, and count my riches gain.
For know, my soul's best treasure, I have
        wealth
Enough to glut ev'n avarice itself.
No more shall cruel want, or proud contempt,
Oppress the sinking spirits, or insult   140
The hoary heads of those who gave me being.
    Char. 'Tis now, O riches, I conceive your
        worth:
You are not base, nor can you be superfluous,
But when misplac'd in base and sordid hands.
Fly, fly, my Wilmot ! Leave thy happy Charlot ! 145
Thy filial piety, the sighs and tears
Of thy lamenting parents call thee hence.
    Y. Wilm. I have a friend, the partner of my
        voyage,
Who, in the storm last night was shipwrack'd
        with me.
    Char. Shipwrack't last night ! — O you im-
        mortal powers !   150

What have you suffer'd! How was you pre-
 serv'd?
 Y. Wilm. Let that, and all my other strange
  escapes
And perilous adventures, be the theme
Of many a happy winter night to come!
My present purpose was t'intreat my angel 155
To know this friend, this other better Wilmot,
And come with him this evening to my father's.
I'll send him to thee.
 Char.   I consent with pleasure.
 Y. Wilm. Heavens! what a night! How
  shall I bear my joy!
My parents, yours, my friends, all will be mine, 160
And mine, like water, air, or the free splendid
  sun,
The undivided portion of you all.
If such the early hopes, the vernal bloom,
The distant prospect of my future bliss:
Then what the ruddy autumn, what the fruit, 165
The full possession of thy heavenly charms!

 The tedious, dark, and stormy winter o'er;
 The hind, that all its pinching hardships bore,

161–162 *And mine, like water . . . you all.* 1783 omits.
165 *autumn . . . fruit.* The editions interpunctuate: *autumn!*
What the fruit!
166 *of thy heavenly charms.* After these words 1783 has the
stage-direction *Exeunt severally*, and omits the remainder of Young
Wilmot's speech; but it is printed in 1775 and 1810.

With transport sees the weeks appointed bring
The chearful, promis'd, gay, delightful spring; 170
The painted meadows, the harmonious woods,
The gentle zephyrs, and unbridled floods,
With all their charms, his ravished thoughts
     employ,
But the rich harvest must compleat his joy.

[*Exeunt.*]

SCENE II.

A Street in Penryn.

Enter Randal.

Randal. Poor, poor, and friendless, whither
     shall I wander,
And to what point direct my views and hopes?—
A menial servant? No! What! Shall I live,
Here in this land of freedom, live distinguished
And marked the willing slave of some proud
     subject, 5
And swell his useless train for broken fragments,
The cold remains of his superfluous board?
I wou'd aspire to something more and better!
Turn thy eyes, then, to the prolifick ocean,
Whose spacious bosom opens to thy view. 10
There, deathless honour and unenvied wealth
Have often crowned the brave adventurer's toils.
This is the native uncontested right,
The fair inheritance of ev'ry Briton

That dares put in his claim. My choice is made : 15
A long farewel to Cornwall, and to England!
If I return, — but stay, what stranger's this,
Who, as he views me, seems to mend his pace ?

Enter Young Wilmot.

Young Wilmot. Randal ! the dear companion
of my youth !
Sure, lavish fortune means to give me all 20
I could desire, or ask for, this blest day,
And leave me nothing to expect hereafter.

Rand. Your pardon, sir ! I know but one on
earth
Cou'd properly salute me by the title
You're pleased to give me, and I would not think 25
That you are he — that you are Wilmot. —

Y. Wilm.   Why ?

Rand. Because I cou'd not bear the disappointment,
Shou'd I be deceived.

Y. Wilm.   I am pleas'd to hear it.
Thy friendly fears better express thy thoughts
Than words could do.

Rand.   O Wilmot ! O my master ! 30
Are you returned ?

Y. Wilm.   I have not yet embraced
My parents ; I shall see you at my father's.

Rand. No, I'm discharged from thence —
O sir ! such ruin —

   Y. Wilm. I've heard it all, and hasten to
    relieve 'em.
Sure, Heaven hath blest me to that very end.   35
I've wealth enough; nor shalt thou want a part.
   Rand. I have a part already: I am blest
In your success, and share in all your joys.
   Y. Wilm. I doubt it not. But tell me, dost
    thou think,
My parents not suspecting my return,   40
That I may visit them, and not be known?
   Rand. 'Tis hard for me to judge. You are
    already
Grown so familiar to me, that I wonder
I knew you not at first. Yet it may be;
For you're much alter'd, and they think you
    dead.   45
   Y. Wilm. This is certain: Charlot beheld me
    long,
And heard my loud reproaches and complaints,
Without rememb'ring she had ever seen me.
My mind at ease grows wanton; I wou'd fain
Refine on happiness. Why may I not   50
Indulge my curiosity, and try
If it be possible, by seeing first
My parents as a stranger, to improve
Their pleasure by surprize?
   Rand.   It may indeed
Inhance your own, to see from what despair   55

Your timely coming and unhoped success
Have given you power to raise them.
  Y. Wilm.   I remember,
E'er since we learned together you excelled
In writing fairly, and could imitate
Whatever hand you saw with great exactness. 60
Of this I'm not so absolute a master.
I therefore beg you'll write, in Charlot's name
And character, a letter to my father;
And recommend me, as a friend of hers,
To his acquaintance.
  Rand.   Sir, if you desire it;—— 65
And yet ——
  Y. Wilm. Nay, no objections! 'Twill save
   time,
Most precious with me now. For the decep-
   tion——
If doing what my Charlot will approve,
'Cause done for me and with a good intent,
Deserves the name —— I'll answer it my self. 70
If this succeeds, I purpose to defer
Discov'ring who I am till Charlot comes,
And thou, and all who love me. Ev'ry friend
Who witnesses my happiness to night,
Will, by partaking, multiply my joys. 75
  Rand. You grow luxurious in your mental
   pleasures.

   76 *your mental pleasures.* 1783, imagination.

Cou'd I deny you aught, I would not write
This letter. To say true, I ever thought
Your boundless curiosity a weakness.
 Y. Wilm. What canst thou blame in this?
 Rand.   Your pardon, sir ! 80
I only speak in general ; I'm ready
T'obey your orders.
 Y. Wilm.   I am much thy debtor;
But I shall find a time to quit thy kindness.
O Randal, but imagine to thyself
The floods of transport, the sincere delight, 85
That all my friends will feel, when I disclose
To my astonished parents my return ;
And then confess, that I have well contrived
By giving others joy t'exalt my own !

 As pain, and anguish, in a gen'rous mind, 90
 While kept concealed and to ourselves con-
   fined,
 Want half their force ; so pleasure when it
   flows
 In torrents round us more extatick grows.
        Exeunt.

 81 *I only speak in general.* 1783, Perhaps I spoke too freely.
90-93 *As pain . . . Exeunt.* 1783 omits.

Scene III

A Room in Old Wilmot's House. Old Wilmot and Agnes.

Old Wilmot. Here, take this Seneca, this haughty pedant,
Who, governing the master of mankind
And awing power imperial, prates of — patience,
And praises poverty, possess'd of millions:
— Sell him, and buy us bread! The scantiest meal   5
The vilest copy of his book e'er purchased,
Will give us more relief in this distress,
Than all his boasted precepts. — Nay, no tears!
Keep them to move compassion when you beg!
    Agnes. My heart may break, but never stoop to that.   10
    O. Wilm. Nor would I live to see it. — But dispatch.   *Exit Agnes.*
Where must I charge this length of misery,
That gathers force each moment as it rolls
And must at last o'erwhelm me, but on hope —
Vain, flattering, delusive, groundless hope —   15
A senseless expectation of relief
That has for years deceived me? Had I thought,

Scene III.   1737, wrongly, Scene II.
16 *A senseless . . . relief.* 1783 omits.

As I do now, as wise men ever think,
When first this hell of poverty o'ertook me,
That power to die implies a right to do it,⠀⠀⠀20
And shou'd be used when life becomes a pain,
What plagues had I prevented! True, my wife
Is still a slave to prejudice and fear.
I would not leave my better part, the dear,

⠀⠀⠀⠀⠀⠀⠀⠀⠀⠀⠀⠀⠀*Weeps.*

Faithful companion of my happier days,⠀⠀⠀25
To bear the weight of age and want alone.
—I'll try once more—

⠀⠀⠀*Enter Agnes, and after her Young Wilmot.*

⠀⠀*O. Wilm.*⠀⠀Returned, my life? So soon?—
⠀⠀*Agn.* The unexpected coming of this stranger
Prevents my going yet.
⠀⠀⠀*Young Wilmot.*⠀⠀⠀You're, I presume,
The gentleman to whom this letter is directed.⠀30

⠀⠀⠀⠀⠀⠀⠀⠀⠀⠀⠀⠀*Gives a letter.*

[*Aside.*] What wild neglect, the token of despair,
What indigence, what misery appears
In each disorder'd, or disfurnished room
Of this once gorgeous house! What discontent,
What anguish and confusion, fill the faces⠀⠀⠀35
Of its dejected owners!
⠀⠀⠀*O. Wilm.*⠀⠀⠀⠀⠀Sir, such welcome

⠀⠀33 *In each disorder'd . . . room.* 1783 omits.
⠀⠀34 *Of this once gorgeous.* 1783, In this once happy.
⠀⠀36 *O. Wilm.* 1783 inserts the direction: [*Having read the letter.*]

Ou... er fri...endly neighbour — o...
T'have called fair Charlot by a dea...
But we have done with hope. I pray, exc...
This incoherence! We had once a son —

Weeps.

   Agn. That you are come from that dear vir-
     tuous maid,
Revives in us the mem'ry of a loss,
Which, tho' long since, we have not learned to
     bear.

   Y. Wilm. (*aside*). The joy to see them, and
     the bitter pain   45
It is to see them thus, touches my soul
With tenderness and grief that will o'erflow.
My bosom heaves and swells, as it would burst;
My bowels move, and my heart melts within
     me.
— They know me not; and yet, I fear, I shall 50
Defeat my purpose and betray myself.

   O. Wilm. The lady calls you here her valued
     friend —
Enough, tho' nothing more should be implied,
To recommend you to our best esteem
— A worthless acquisition! May she find 55
Some means that better may express her kind-
     ness!

48–49 *My bosom . . . within me.* 1783 omits.
50 *I fear, I shall.* 1783, I shall I fear.

But she, perhaps, hath purpose
You with herself, and end her fru   ...sorrow
For one whom death alone can justify
For leaving her so long? If it be so   60
May you repair his loss, and be to Charlot
A second, happier Wilmot! Partial nature,
Who only favours youth, as feeble age
Were not her offspring or below her care,
Has seal'd our doom: no second hope shall
     spring   65
From my dead loins and Agnes' steril womb,
To dry our tears, and dissipate despair.

    Agn. The last and most abandon'd of our kind,
By Heaven and earth neglected or despised,
The loathsom grave, that robb'd us of our son   70
And all our joys in him, must be our refuge.

    Y. Wilm. Let ghosts unpardon'd or devoted
     fiends,
Fear without hope, and wail in such sad strains;
But grace defend the living from despair!
The darkest hours precede the rising sun,   75
And mercy may appear when least expected.

    O. Wilm. This I have heard a thousand
     times repeated,
And have, believing, been as oft deceived.

    Y. Wilm. Behold in me an instance of its
     truth!

     66 *From my dead . . . steril womb.* 1783 omits.

At sea twice shipwrack'd, and
Of lawless pyrates; by the Arabs
Surpriz'd and robb'd on shore; and once
To worse than these, the sum of all distress
That the most wretched feel on this side hell,
Ev'n slavery itself — yet, here I stand,   85
Except one trouble that will quickly end,
The happiest of mankind.

    O. Wilm.   A rare example
Of fortune's caprice, apter to surprize,
Or entertain, than comfort or instruct.
If you wou'd reason from events, be just,   90
And count, when you escaped, how many per-
        ished;
And draw your inf'rence thence!
    Agn.   Alas! who knows
But we were rendred childless by some storm,
In which you, tho' preserv'd, might bear a part.
    Y. Wilm. (*aside*). How has my curiosity be-
        tray'd me   95
Into superfluous pain! I faint with fondness,
And shall, if I stay longer, rush upon 'em,
Proclaim myself their son, kiss and embrace 'em,
Till their souls, transported with the excess
Of pleasure and surprize, quit their frail man-
        sions,   100

    99–100 *Till their souls . . . mansions.* 1783:
        Till, with the excess of pleasure and surprize,
        Their souls, transported, their frail mansions quit.

And leave 'em breathless in my longing arms.
By circumstances then and slow degrees,
They must be let into a happiness
Too great for them to bear at once and live.
That Charlot will perform. I need not feign   105
To ask an hour for rest. — Sir, I intreat
The favour to retire, where for a while
I may repose my self. You will excuse
This freedom, and the trouble that I give you :
'Tis long since I have slept, and nature calls.   110

    O. Wilm. I pray, no more ! Believe, we're
        only troubled,
That you shou'd think any excuse were need-
        ful.

    Y. Wilm. The weight of this is some incum-
        brance to me,

      Takes a casket out of his bosom and gives it
      to his mother.

And its contents of value. If you please
To take the charge of it 'till I awake,   115
I shall not rest the worse. If I shou'd sleep
'Till I am ask'd for, as perhaps I may,
I beg that you wou'd wake me.

    Agn.   Doubt it not !
Distracted as I am with various woes,
I shall remember that.   *Exit.*

    Y. Wilm.   Merciless grief !   120

  120 *I shall remember that.* 1783 adds, *Exit, with Old Wilmot.*

What ravage has it made ? how has
Her lovely form and mind ! I feel her an
And dread I know not what from her despair.
My father too — O grant 'em patience, Heaven!
A little longer, a few short hours more,   125
And all their cares, and mine, shall end for ever.

    How near is misery and joy ally'd;
    Nor eye nor thought can their extreams
        divide !
    A moment's space is long, and light'ning
        slow,
    To fate descending to reverse our woe,   130
    Or blast our hopes and all our joys o'er-
        throw.   *Exeunt.*

126 *end for ever.* 1783, *Aside, Exeunt.*
127–131 *How near . . . o'erthrow. Exeunt.* 1783 omits.

Act III.

Scene I. *The scene continued.*

Enter Agnes, alone, with the casket in her hand.

Agnes. Who shou'd this stranger be? And
    then, this casket!
He says it is of value, and yet trusts it,
As if a trifle, to a stranger's hand.
His confidence amazes me. Perhaps
It is not what he says. I'm strongly tempted   5
To open it, and see — no, let it rest!
Why should my curiosity excite me
To search and pry into th'affairs of others,
Who have, t'imploy my thoughts, so many cares
And sorrows of my own? — With how much
    ease   10
The spring gives way! Surprizing! most pro-
    digious!
My eyes are dazzled, and my ravished heart
Leaps at the glorious sight. How bright's the
    lustre,
How immense the worth of these fair jewels!
Ay, such a treasure would expel for ever   15
Base poverty and all its abject train;

7 *Why should . . . excite me.* 1783 omits.
8–11 *To search . . . prodigious!* 1783:
      Why should I pry into the cares of others,
      Who have so many sorrows of my own?
      With how much ease the spring gives way — surprizing!—

The mean devices we're reduced to use
To keep out famine, and preserve our lives
From day to day; the cold neglect of friends;
The galling scorn, or more provoking pity   20
Of an insulting world — possess'd of these,
Plenty, content and power might take their turn,
And lofty pride bare its aspiring head
At our approach, and once more bend before us.
— A pleasing dream! — 'Tis past; and now I
    wake,   25
More wretched by the happiness I've lost.
For, sure, it was a happiness to think,
Tho' but a moment, such a treasure mine!
Nay, it was more than thought: I saw and
    touched
The bright temptation, and I see it yet.   30
'Tis here—'tis mine—I have it in possession—
Must I resign it? Must I give it back?
Am I in love with misery and want,
To rob myself, and court so vast a loss?
—Return it, then!—But how? There is a way—   35
Why sinks my heart? Why does my blood run
    cold?
Why am I thrill'd with horror? 'Tis not choice,
But dire necessity, suggests the thought.

17–21 *The mean devices . . . world.* Instead of this passage,
1783 reads:

    Famine; the cold neglect of friends; the scorn,
    Or more provoking pity of the world.

Enter Old Wilmot.

Old Wilmot. The mind contented, with how
    little pains
The wand'ring senses yield to soft repose,   40
And die to gain new life ! He's fallen asleep
Already — happy man ! What dost thou think,
My Agnes, of our unexpected guest ?
He seems to me a youth of great humanity.
Just e're he closed his eyes, that swam in tears, 45
He wrung my hand and pressed it to his lips,
And, with a look that pierced me to the soul,
Begg'd me to comfort thee, and — dost thou
    hear me ? —
What art thou gazing on ? Fie ! 'tis not well.
This casket was deliver'd to you closed ;   50
Why have you open'd it ? Shou'd this be known,
How mean must we appear !
   Agn.   And who shall know it ?
   O. Wilm. There is a kind of pride, a decent
    dignity
Due to our selves, which, spite of our misfor-
    tunes,
May be maintain'd and cherish'd to the last.   55
To live without reproach, and without leave
To quit the world, shews sovereign contempt
And noble scorn of its relentless malice.

41 *And die to gain new life.* 1783 omits, reading for what follows :
     He 's fallen asleep already — Happy man !
     What dost thou think, my Agnes, of our guest ?

Agn. Shews sovereign madness and a scorn
    of sense !
Pursue no farther this detested theme !   60
I will not die, I will not leave the world,
For all that you can urge, until compell'd.
    O. Wilm. To chace a shadow, when the
        setting sun
Is darting his last rays, were just as wise
As your anxiety for fleeting life,   65
Now the last means for its support are failing.
Were famine not as mortal as the sword,
This warmth might be excused. But take thy
    choice :
Die how you will, you shall not die alone.
    Agn. Nor live, I hope.
    O. Wilm.   There is no fear of that. 70
    Agn. Then, we'll live both.
    O. Wilm.   Strange folly ! where's the means ?
    Agn. The means are there ; those jewels —
    O. Wilm.   Ha ! — Take heed !
Perhaps thou dost but try me ; yet, take heed !
There's nought so monstrous but the mind of
    man
In some conditions may be brought t'approve : 75
Theft, sacrilege, treason, and parricide,
When flatt'ring opportunity enticed
And desperation drove, have been committed

68 *This warmth.* 1783, Your warmth.
72 *The means are.* 1783 omits, Agnes replying: There : those.

By those who once wou'd start to hear them
          named.

  Agn. And add to these detested suicide, 80
Which, by a crime much less, we may avoid.

   O. Wilm. Th' inhospitable murder of our
          guest !—
How cou'dst thou form a thought so very
          tempting,
So advantageous, so secure, and easy,
And yet so cruel, and so full of horror? 85

  Agn. 'Tis less impiety, less against nature,
To take another's life, than end our own.

  O. Wilm. It is no matter, whether this or that
Be, in itself, the less or greater crime.
Howe'er we may deceive our selves or others, 90
We act from inclination, not by rule,
Or none could act amiss; and, that all err,
None but the conscious hypocrite denies.
—O! what is man, his excellence and strength,
When in an hour of trial and desertion, 95
Reason, his noblest power, may be suborned
To plead the cause of vile assassination!

  Agn. You're too severe: Reason may justly
          plead
For her own preservation.

   O. Wilm.   Rest contented!

  82 *Th'inhospitable . . . guest.* 1783 omits.
  83 *tempting.* 1783, damning.
  88 *It is . . . that.* 1783, No matter which, the less or greater
crime. 89 *Be, in itself . . . crime.* 1783 omits.

Whate'er resistance I may seem to make,   100
I am betray'd within; my will's seduced,
And my whole soul infected. The desire
Of life returns, and brings with it a train
Of appetites, that rage to be supplied.
Whoever stands to parley with temptation,   105
Does it to be o'ercome.

Agn.   Then, nought remains,
But the swift execution of a deed
That is not to be thought on, or delay'd.
We must dispatch him sleeping: shou'd he wake,
'Twere madness to attempt it.

O. Wilm.   True, his strength, 110
Single, is more, much more than ours united;
So may his life, perhaps, as far exceed
Ours in duration, shou'd he 'scape this snare.
Gen'rous, unhappy man! O! what cou'd move
        thee
To put thy life and fortune in the hands   115
Of wretches mad with anguish?

Agn.   By what means —
By stabbing, suffocation, or by strangling —
Shall we effect his death?

O. Wilm.   Why, what a fiend!
How cruel, how remorseless and impatient,
Have pride and poverty made thee!

109–110 *We must . . . attempt it.* 1783 omits.
110–113 *True, his strength . . . this snare.* 1783 omits.
117 *By stabbing . . . strangling.* 1783 omits.

Agn.   Barbarous man ! 120
Whose wasteful riots ruin'd our estate,
And drove our son, ere the first down had spread
His rosy cheeks, spite of my sad presages,
Earnest intreaties, agonies and tears,
To seek his bread 'mongst strangers, and to perish 125
In some remote, inhospitable land —
The loveliest youth, in person and in mind,
That ever crown'd a groaning mother's pains !
Where was thy pity, where thy patience then ?
Thou cruel husband ! thou unnat'ral father !   130
Thou most remorseless, most ungrateful man :
To waste my fortune, rob me of my son,
To drive me to despair, and then reproach me
For being what thou'st made me !
    O. Wilm.   Dry thy tears ;
I ought not to reproach thee. I confess   135
That thou hast suffer'd much. So have we both.
But chide no more ; I'm wrought up to thy
                purpose.
The poor, ill-fated, unsuspecting victim,
Ere he reclined him on the fatal couch,
From which he's ne'er to rise, took off the sash 140
And costly dagger that thou saw'st him wear,
And thus, unthinking, furnish'd us with arms
Against himself. Which shall I use ?
    Agn.   The sash.
If you make use of that, I can assist.

143–146 *Which shall I use . . . the guilt.* 1783 omits.

O. *Wilm.*   No!
'Tis a dreadful office, and I'll spare   145
Thy trembling hands the guilt. Steal to the door,
And bring me word if he be still asleep.

                              Ex[*it*] *Ag*[*nes*].

Or I'm deceiv'd, or he pronounc'd himself
The happiest of mankind. Deluded wretch!
Thy thoughts are perishing; thy youthful joys, 150
Touch'd by the icy hand of grisly death,
Are with'ring in their bloom. — But, thought
          extinguisht,
He'll never know the loss, nor feel the bitter
Pangs of disappointment. — Then I was wrong
In counting him a wretch. To die well pleas'd, 155
Is all the happiest of mankind can hope for;
To be a wretch, is to survive the loss
Of every joy, and even hope itself,
As I have done. Why do I mourn him, then?
For, by the anguish of my tortur'd soul,   160
He's to be envy'd, if compar'd with me.

     Enter Agnes with Young Wilmot's dagger.

     Agn. The stranger sleeps at present; but so
          restless

162 *The stranger . . . restless.* 1737 and 1810 print, regardless
of the metre :

                    The stranger
          Sleeps at present ; but so restless, etc.

     Below, they print *Nay for shame . . . be more your self* as one
line, and *You're quite dismay'd . . . deed my self* as two lines,
broken at *do*; and, with 1775, break *Give me . . . single murther*
at *steel.*

His slumbers seem, they can't continue long.
Come, come, dispatch! — Here, I've secur'd
    his dagger.
   O. Wilm. O Agnes! Agnes! if there be a
    hell, 'tis just   165
We shou'd expect it.
               Goes to take the dagger but lets it fall.
   Agn.   Nay, for shame!
Shake off this panick, and be more your self!
   O. Wilm. What's to be done? On what had
    we determin'd?
   Agn. You're quite dismay'd; I'll do the deed
    my self.   *Takes up the dagger.*
   O. Wilm. Give me the fatal steel.—'Tis but
    a single murther   170
Necessity, impatience and despair,
The three wide mouths of that true Cerberus,
Grim poverty, demands.—They shall be stopp'd.
Ambition, persecution, and revenge
Devour their millions daily; and shall I —   175
But follow me, and see how little cause
You had to think there was the least remains
Of manhood, pity, mercy, or remorse
Left in this savage breast! *Going the wrong way.*
   Agn.   Where do you go?
The street is that way.

164 *Come, come, dispatch.* 1783 omits.
166 *Nay, for shame.* 1783 omits.
169 *I'll do the deed my self.* 1783 omits.
173 *demands.* 1783, demand.

O. Wilm.   True! I had forgot.   180

Agn. Quite, quite confounded!

O. Wilm. Well, I recover. — I shall find the
    way.   *Exit.*

Agn. O softly! softly! The least noise un-
    does us.

Still I fear him. — No! now he seems deter-
    min'd!

O! that pause! that cowardly pause! His
    resolution fails —   185

'Tis wisely done to lift your eyes to Heaven.

When did you pray before? — I have no pa-
    tience —

How he surveys him! What a look was there—

How full of anguish, pity and remorse!

—He'll never do it. — Strike, or give it o'er! —190

—No, he recovers. — But that trembling arm

---

182 *Well, I recover, etc.* The following lines are arranged
without much attention to metre in all the editions which seem
generally to follow the arrangement of 1737 :

> *O. Wilm.* Well, I recover.
> — I shall find the way.
>   *Agn.* O softly! Softly!
> The least noise undoes us.
> — Still I fear him :
> — No, now he seems determin'd — O! that pause.

184 *Still I fear him . . . O Wilmot! Wilmot.* 1783 omits.

185 *O! that pause!* All editions read : *O! that pause.*

> *His resolution fails.* After this, 1783 reads :

> What are we doing? Misery and want
> Are lighter ills than this — I cannot bear it!
> Stop! hold thy hand! inconstant, wretched woman!
> What! doth my heart recoil? O Wilmot! Wilmot!
> What pow'r shall I invoke to aid thee, Wilmot?

May miss its aim; and if he fails, we're lost.
'Tis done — O, no! he lives, he struggles yet!

Y. Wilm. (*in another room*). O, father! father!

Agn.   Quick, repeat the blow!
What pow'r shall I invoke to aid thee, Wilmot? 195
—Yet, hold thy hand! — Inconstant, wretched
          woman!
What! doth my heart recoil, and bleed with him
Whose murder you contrived? — O Wilmot!
          Wilmot!   [*Exit.*]

Enter Charlot, Maria, Eustace, Randal and others.

Charlot. What strange neglect! The doors
          are all unbarr'd,
And not a living creature to be seen.   200

Enter Old Wilmot and Agnes.

Char. Sir, we are come to give and to receive
A thousand greetings. — Ha! what can this
          mean?
Why do you look with such amazement on us?
Are these your transports for your son's return?
Where is my Wilmot? Has he not been here? 205
Wou'd he defer your happiness so long,
Or cou'd a habit so disguise your son,
That you refus'd to own him?

Agn.   Heard you that?
What prodigy of horror is disclosing,
To render murther venial?

Maria. 1783 omits.   *and others.* 1783 omits.

O. Wilm.   Prithee, peace!   210
The miserable damn'd suspend their howling,
And the swift orbs are fixt in deep attention.

   Y. Wilm. (*groans*). Oh! oh! oh!

   Eustace. Sure that deep groan came from the
      inner room.

   Randal. It did; and seem'd the voice of one
      expiring.   215
Merciful Heaven, where will these terrors end?
That is the dagger my young master wore;
And see, his father's hands are stained with
      blood!   *Young Wilmot groans again.*

   Eust. Another groan! Why do we stand to
      gaze
On these dumb phantoms of despair and horror? 220
Let us search farther: Randal, shew the way.

   Char. This is the third time those fantastick
      forms
Have forc'd themselves upon my mental eyes,

213–215 *Y. Wilm.* (*groans*) . . . *expiring.* 1783 omits.

216 *Merciful Heaven . . . end.* 1783 reads:

        What mean these dreadful words?

218 *And see . . . groans again.* 1783 omits.

219 *Another groan . . . gaze.* 1783 reads instead of this line:

        My mind misgives me.
        Do not stand to gaze.

221 *shew the way.* 1783 inserts [*Exeunt.*

222 *Char. This is the third time.* 1783 omits Charlot's speech
and all that follows to *endless perturbation*; and then adds: *Manent
Old Wilmot and Agnes.*

And sleeping gave me more than waking pains.
O you eternal pow'rs! if all your mercy　　225
To wretched mortals be not quite extinguish'd,
And terrors only guard your awful thrones,
Remove this dreadful vision; let me wake,
Or sleep the sleep of death!

　　　　Exeunt Charlot, Maria, Eustace, Randal, &c.

　　O. Wilm.　　　　　　Sleep those who may!
I know my lot is endless perturbation.　　230
　　Agn. Let life forsake the earth, and light the
　　　　sun,
And death and darkness bury in oblivion
Mankind and all their deeds, that no posterity
May ever rise to hear our horrid tale,
Or view the grave of such detested parricides!　235
　　O. Wilm. Curses and deprecations are in vain:
The sun will shine, and all things have their
　　　　course,
When we, the curse and burthen of the earth,
Shall be absorb'd and mingled with its dust.
Our guilt and desolation must be told　　240
From age to age, to teach desponding mortals,
How far beyond the reach of human thought
Heaven, when incens'd, can punish.—Die thou
　　　　first!
I dare not trust thy weakness.　　*Stabs Agnes.*
　　Agn.　　　　　　　Ever kind,
But most in this.

O. Wilm.   I will not long survive thee. 245

Agn.   Do not accuse thy erring mother, Wilmot,

With too much rigour when we meet above!

Rivers of tears, and ages spent in howling

Cou'd ne'er express the anguish of my heart.

To give thee life for life, and blood for blood,   250

Is not enough.   Had I ten thousand lives,

I'd give them all to speak my penitence,

Deep, and sincere, and equal to my crime.   *Dies.*

     Enter Charlot led by Maria, and Randal; Eustace,
              and the rest.

    Charlot.   Welcome, despair! I'll never hope
       again.

Why have you forced me from my Wilmot's side? 255

Let me return — unhand me — let me die!

Patience, that till this moment ne'er forsook me,

Has took her flight; and my abandon'd mind,

Rebellious to a lot so void of mercy

And so unexpected, rages to madness.   260

—O thou, who know'st our frame, who know'st
        these woes

Are more than human fortitude can bear,

O take me, take me hence, e're I relapse;

And in distraction, with unhallow'd tongue,

Again arraign your mercy! —   *Faints.* 265

    248–249 *Rivers . . . heart.* 1783 omits.

     Enter Charlot . . . rest. 1783 reads: Enter Randal, Eustace;
and omits all that follows, down to *vent my grief,* l. 268.

Eust. Unhappy maid ! This strange event my
    strength
Can scarce support; no wonder thine should
    fail.
— How shall I vent my grief ? O Wilmot !
    Wilmot !
Thou truest lover, and thou best of friends,
Are these the fruits of all thy anxious cares   270
For thy ungrateful parents ? — Cruel fiends,
To use thee thus, to recompense with death
Thy most unequall'd duty and affection !

   O. Wilm. What whining fool art thou, who
    would'st usurp
My sovereign right of grief ? Was he thy son ? 275
Say, canst thou shew thy hands reeking with
    blood,
That flow'd, thro' purer channels, from thy
    loins ?

   Eust. Forbid it, Heaven, that I should know
    such guilt ;
Yet his sad fate demands commiseration.

   O. Wilm. Compute the sands that bound the
    spacious ocean,   280
And swell their number with a single grain ;
Increase the noise of thunder with thy voice ;

---

269 *Thou truest . . . friends.* 1783 omits.
272–273 *To use thee thus . . . affection.* 1783 omits.
278 *Forbid it, Heaven.* 1783 omits this and the following line.

Or, when the raging wind lays nature waste,
Assist the tempest with thy feeble breath;
Add water to the sea, and fire to Etna;   285
But name not thy faint sorrow with the anguish
Of a curst wretch who only hopes for this —

                        Stabbing himself.

To change the scene, but not relieve his pain!
   Rand. A dreadful instance of the last re-
      morse!
May all your woes end here!
   O. Wilm.   O would they end 290
A thousand ages hence, I then should suffer
Much less than I deserve. Yet let me say,
You'll do but justice, to inform the world:
This horrid deed, that punishes itself,
Was not intended as he was our son;   295
For that we knew not, 'till it was too late.
Proud and impatient under our afflictions,
While Heaven was labouring to make us happy,
We brought this dreadful ruin on ourselves.
Mankind may learn — but — oh! —   *Dies.*
   Rand.   The most will not : 300

---

295 *as he was our son.* 1783, thinking him our son.

300–306 *The most . . . too soon.* 1783 omits, with the final
Exeunt. In the place of these lines 1783 reads :

> *Rand.* Heaven grant they may,
>   And may thy penitence atone thy crime !
>   Tend well thy hapless Charlot, and bear hence
>   These bleeding victims of despair and pride !
>   Toll the death bell, and follow to the grave
>   The wretched Parents and ill-fated Son.

Let us at least be wiser, nor complain
Of Heaven's mysterious ways, and awful
    reign.
By our bold censures we invade his throne
Who made mankind, and governs but his own.
Tho' youthful Wilmot's sun be set e're noon, 305
The ripe in virtue never die too soon.

                                Exeunt.

FINIS.

Notes to Fatal Curiosity

141. Prologue, written by Henry Feilding, Esq., Spoken by Mr. Roberts. Roberts, who played Old Wilmot in the first production of the piece, does not appear to have been an actor of much contemporary note.

141, 1. The Tragic Muse, etc. Cf. the opening of the Younger Cibber's *Prologue* to *The London Merchant*.

141, 2. With Shakespeare's nature, or with Fletcher's ease. Dryden sufficiently exposed this kind of would-be discriminating judgment. See his *Prologue to the Tempest* (1667):

> 'Shakespeare, who, taught by none, did first impart
> To Fletcher wit, to labouring Jonson art;
> He, monarch-like, gave those his subjects law,
> And is that Nature which they paint and draw.'

See also the *Preface to Troilus and Cressida* (1679), in one passage of which he says that, in the matter of making generally apparent the manners of his persons, Fletcher comes far short of Shakespeare, as indeed he does almost in everything; while in another passage Dryden concludes that Fletcher, after all, 'was a limb of Shakespeare.'

141, 6. Each single character might speak them all. Cf. John Sheffield, Duke of Buckinghamshire's *Essay on Satire*:

> 'And even fools speak sense, as if possest,
> And each by inspiration breaks his jest.'

141, 14. without: outside, beyond.

141, 16. And tho' our little stage as yet be young. The New, or Little, Theatre in the Haymarket had been opened in 1723, having apparently been built on speculation, and was carried on in a more or less hand-to-mouth fashion till Fielding took it in 1736, when he opened it with his *Pasquin*.

143. Prologue, Written by George Colman, 1782. Spoken by Mr. Palmer. This was John Palmer, who performed the part of Young Wilmot on the occasion. He was an actor of extraordinary versatility (up to a certain point, apparently), as is shown by the 'selected' list of his characters in Genest, VII, 344–350.

146. Dramatis Personae. The edition of 1782 adds the following list of actors of the above characters in 1782:

Old Wilmot	Beasley
Young Wilmot	Palmer
Eustace	R. Palmer
Randal	J. Bannister
Agnes	Miss Sherry
Charlot	Mrs. Bulkley
Maria	Miss Hooke

147, 3. Nor no time decaying. For examples of the double negative, an idiom which 'is a very natural one, and quite common in Elizabethan English,' see Abbott's *Shakesperean Grammar.*

147, 10. Posts: hastens.

147, 12. The sad prerogative above him: the sad prerogative which is beyond him; to which he is unequal.

149, 30. The brave Sir Walter Raleigh, etc. Raleigh arrived at Plymouth about the middle of June, 1618. Soon afterwards he started for London, but was arrested at Ashburton by his cousin, Sir Lewis Stukeley, who took him back to Plymouth. Orders were then sent for him to be taken to London; and here, when attempting to escape to France *via* Gravesend, he was finally arrested and consigned to the Tower. King James's promise to give him up or have him hanged in England, was given on June 25th.

149, 38. There's now no insolence that Spain can offer, etc. *Fatal Curiosity* was produced in 1736, when there was already great tension in the relations between England and Spain. The story— or fable — of 'Jenkins's ear' was revived, and set the country aflame, early in 1738. 'This Jenkins had been master of a trading sloop from Jamaica, which was boarded and searched by a Spanish Guarda Costa, and though no proofs of smuggling were discovered, yet, according to his own statement, he underwent the most barbarous usage. The Spanish Captain, he said, had torn off one of his ears, bidding him carry it to his King, and tell His Majesty that were he present he should be treated in the same manner. This story, which had lain dormant for seven years, was now [1738] seasonably revived at the bar of the House of Commons. It is certain that Jenkins had lost an ear, or part of an ear, which he always carried about with him wrapped in cotton to display to his audience; but I find it alleged by no mean authority, that he had lost it on another occasion, and perhaps, as seems to be insinuated, in the pillory. His tale, however, as always happens in moments of great excitement, was readily admitted without proof; and a spirited answer which he gave enhanced the popular effect. Being asked by a Member what were his feelings when he found himself in the hands of such barbarians, " I recommended," said he, " my soul to God, and my cause to my country." These words flew rapidly from mouth to mouth, adding fuel to the general flame, and it is almost incredible how strong an impulse was imparted both to Parliament and to the public. " We have no need of allies to enable us to command justice," cried Pulteney; " the story of Jenkins will raise volunteers." ' *History of England from the Peace of Utrecht*, Lord Mahon (Earl Stanhope), 1839, ii, 403–04.

Lillo's Dutch origin no doubt contributed to his Hispanophobia. See *Introduction*, as to his *Britannia and Batavia*.

149, 51. I saw her pass the High street towards the Minster. See *Introduction*.

153, 133–34.

> Quit books and the unprofitable search
> Of wisdom there, and study human-kind.

Cf. the maxim imparted by Mephistophiles to the Student in *Faust*:

> ' All theory, my worthy friend, is grey,
> And green the golden tree of life.'

156, 11. There is in melody a secret charm, etc. The idea is much the same as that of the opening lines of *Twelfth Night*.

162, 137. But by: By but.

162, 139. The merit we've been raising: the merit (in the theological sense) we have been accumulating.

167, 3. savage men, etc. The wreckers. See *Introduction*, p. xlviii.

169, 39. most men, etc. It would not be difficult to find illustrations of this fancy, akin to the delight which, according to Izaak Walton, Sir Henry Wotton took in the 'connaturalness of that which he called his "genial air."' The lines which follow are taken from Müller's *Der neunundzwanzigste Februar*, a drama of which, as has been seen, the origin is traceable to *Fatal Curiosity*:

> 'Where it began its growth the tree
> Withers indifferent and perforce;
> The stream flows gaily to the sea,
> Unmindful of its rocky source;
> The planets run their spheric course;
> Akin to heaven's wanderers, man
> Dies happy where his life began.'

179, 80. inhabit'st, a neuter verb. Cf. *Paradise Lost*, II, 355:

> '— to learn
> What creatures there inhabit.'

180, 102. Enlarg'd: set free.

183, 153–54. the theme Of many a happy winter night to come. Cf. the title of Shakespeare's play, and, still more appositely, Marlowe and Nash's *Tragedy of Dido, Queen of Carthage*, Act III, Sc. 3:

> 'Who would not undergo all kind of toil
> To be well-stor'd with such a winter's tale?'

184, 4. distinguished seems merely to mean the same as *marked*.

189, 1. take this Seneca. Whether or not Seneca, who commends the virtue of patience, or at all events that of humility, in his *Epistles*, and doubtless also in his philosophical writings, ever 'awed' his pupil Nero by the excellent principles which he laid down for his education, may be open to doubt. The 'millions,' of which the philosopher was possessed, are stated to have amounted to 300 (of sesterces); and, according to Tacitus, Seneca told the Emperor that so many honours and so much wealth had been accumulated by him upon his tutor that nothing was wanting to the happiness of the recipient of his favours but the moderating of it. (*Ann.* xiv, 53–4.)

189, 12. Where must I charge: On what must I fix the responsibility?

191, 49. My bowels move. *Lamentations*, 1,20, *et al.*

192, 63. as feeble age: as if feeble age.

201, 105. Whoever stands to parley, etc. 'The woman who deliberates is lost.'

202, 122. spread: overspread.

204, 171-73. Necessity, impatience and despair ... demands. This is a striking survival of a form very common in the First Folio of Shakespeare — the third person plural in -*s*. (See Abbott, *Shakesperean Grammar*, 333.)

206, 209. disclosing: disclosing itself.

206, 210. To render murther venial: so as to make mere ordinary murder (as distinct from the murder of a son) seem venial.

207, 212. And the swift orbs, etc. This must mean, either that the roving eyes of the damned are riveted upon this awful spectacle, or that the planets become fixed stars in order to contemplate it. The latter explanation seems on the whole the worse.

210, 274. What whining fool art thou, etc. A palpable imitation of *Hamlet*, Act v, Sc. 1 :

> ' What is he whose grief
> Bears such an emphasis . . . .
> . . . . . . forty-thousand brothers
> Could not, with all their quantity of love,
> Make up my sum.'

211, 295. as he was: as if he had been.

Appendix

I

THE SOURCE OF FATAL CURIOSITY

The following story to which reference has already been made, may with great probability, if not with absolute certainty, be set down as the original source of the plot of *Fatal Curiosity*. It can hardly be a mere coincidence that a similar incident said to have happened at Leipzig, and related in Johann Jakob Vogel's *Leipzigisches Geschichtsbuch*, quoted by Hoffmann, *Schlesische Volkslieder*, is there stated to have happened at Leipzig in 1618 — the year assigned to the 'Perin' murder, and that in which Abraham a Sancta Clara (1704) places another occurrence of the same kind. The Leipzig story is not corroborated by the official registers. Vogel cites Gottfried (Schultz') *Chronica* (1656) as containing the same story, but dating it 1649 and placing its occurrence at Thermels in Bohemia. Similar stories have been traced to Dithmarschen, Mecklenburg, Danzig, and the Grisons. Dunlop (*History of Fiction*, ed. 1845, p. 277) mentions the same story as told by Vincenzo Rota in one of the late *novelle*, written early in the last century, but first printed by Count Borromco as late as 1794, which locates it at Brescia. This story was translated by E. von

Bülow in his *Novellenbuch* (1834). Dunlop says that a similar story, told in *The Visitor* (an English journal), of an innkeeper in Normandy, forms the basis of the plot of Lillo's play. There are two popular German ballads on the subject : *Es hatt ein Gastwirt einen Sohn* and *Es waren einmal zwei Bauernsöhn*; and a Czech ballad resembling the former of these. F. Gregorovius heard a ballad on the same theme in Corsica. A French popular ballad characteristically confines the deed to the mother, not mentioning the father. *Haec quidem hactenus*, though a Bulgarian, apparently a Polish, and a Chinese analogue are likewise noted. (See R. Köhler, and W. E. A. Axon's note, *u.s.*) The following is taken literatim from the copy of the 1618 pamphlet in the Bodleian Library.

NEWES

From Perin in Cornwall

OF

A most Bloody and vn-exampled Murther

very lately committed by a Father on his owne

Sonne (who was lately returned from the Indyes) at

the Instigation of a mercilesse

Step-mother.

Together with their Severall most wretched endes, being

all performed in the Month of Septem-

ber last. Anno 1618.

[Woodcut of the murder.]

LONDON

Printed by E. A. and are to be sold at *Christ-Church*

gate, 1618.

[Woodcut of a coffin.]

An vnfortunate Murther
lately committed neere *Perin*
in *Cornwall*.

AT Perin a Towne in Cornwall, liv'd a man of
honest life and ample possessions : Being in his
youth blest with a vertuous Wife, who brought him many
sweete and toward Children : that stood like so many
Olive branches about his Table : And thus was he a long
time blest, onely because he feared the Lord.

But as there is no day so bright and glorious, in which
one cloud or other interposeth not itselfe, and no estate so
firme but it is subiect to alteration : So it fell out with
him, for amongst the rest, one of his Children, and (which
augmented his griefe the more) the youngest prov'd so
wilde and misgovern'd, as neither gentle admonitions of
his Parents, nor sevearer correction of Maister or Tutor,
could any way worke to good purpose vpon him, so wilde
and rancke grew the weedes of disobedient stubbernnesse
in him : that consorted with a crew of his owne condition,
hauing made what spoyle they could a shore, they determin'd a voyage to Sea, and made what hauocke they
could there also.

Which tooke effect : Being once at Sea (*Dux omnium
malorum* as we terme it) they spare neither Spanish, French,
Dutch, Scotch or English, but make good the Proverbe,
and count all Fish that come to the net : And hauing
(after many petty ones) taken one rich prize, thinking

with the Fools in their hearts that there was no God but
their golde, they determin'd to put a shore in Turkey,
and there lewdly spend what was vnlawfully got :

But marke the Judgement of God vpon such, being
within kenne of shore, they were suddenly becalm'd, and
set vpon by the Turkish Gallyes, who after long and
sharpe fight of both sides, got the better : yet such was
their resolution, they fought it out to the last man, so as
our English Gallant seeing no way to safety, tooke some
of the best and wealthiest Jewels he had about him, and
with his sword in his hand leapt into the Sea.

The Turkes men minding the booty, then our naked
men boarded and fell to rifling, where they found much
wealth, and accordingly enioyed it.

In the meane time our English caveliere, with much
difficultie recouers the shore, where with colde comfort
(we may imagin) seeing he could not saue those thinges,
for which his soule and body were (without God's great
mercy) quite lost, he began to looke back into the past
course of his life, where finding much matter of griefe,
but little or none of any comfort, he began to fall into
serious meditation with himselfe, that if he with the rest
of his comforts had been cast away at Sea, with all his
bloody and vn-repented sinnes about him : viz Theft,
Piracy, Murther, Drunkennes, Swearing, Lust, blasphemy and the like : In what a miserable and desperate
estate his poore forlorne soule should have stood at the
last great and terrible Day : when the sentence of dread-
full *Ite*, and comfortable *Venite*, shall be (by the great

and most high Judge, and chiefe Justice of all Flesh) be pronounced.

But withall, hoping and confessing it was Gods mercy to giue him longer time for repentance, that the Sea had not swallowed him with the rest, he began to gather comfort, and make a Christian vse of his preseruation: in this manner determining to change those Jewels and Diamonds he had, into Golde, and with them turne petty Marchant, or some like honest and thriuing course.

But going to sell his Jewels, it happened that one of the richest was knowne to haue belonged to the Gouernour of the Towne, vnder whose Commaund he then was. The truth of the businesse examin'd, it fell out that the Ship which he and his Company had taken and rifled at Sea, (and in which that Jewell with others were found) belong'd to the Governour of *Argiers*.

In regard whereof, he was presently apprehended as a Pirate and so sentenc'd a slave to the Gallyes: To pleade Excuse, or beg for mercy was in vaine, into a Galley was our gallant conducted, where chayn'd amongst other Christians to the Bogaban't,[1] he was inioyn'd to tugge at an Oare: his Dinner and Supper coarse Bran and water, his morning Breakfast and afternoone Beuer,[2] the Buls pizle and the Bastinado. A good caueat for our fierce heads, whose running wits are some at *Rome*, some in *Venice*, and some in *Spaine*, before their heads be out of the shell.

Now he begins to call to minde his disobedience to his Parents : and thinke what a quiet life and full of pleasure

---

1 Rowing bench.   2 Slight repast, usually between meals.

it had beene for him, to haue sit in his Furd gowne at his study in the Universitie, or warme and dry at some honest Tradesmans shop in the Citty : to haue had warme dyet twice a day and welcome, and not have begg'd coarse Bran and water, and haue gone without it.

These and the like considerations were his familiar discourse: hauing continued some while in the Galley, comming one day a shore,[1] whilest the Captaine and other Officers fell to quaffing : he and other Christians with him (slaues) to the number of some Ten, by their industry fylde off their Irons, and hiding their legges in short strawe that was allow'd them in the night, their Captaine and Officers dranke so a shore and others in the Galley, they made a desperate and yet happy escape, and got a shore, where such luckie successe crowned their attempts, that in few monthes after (assisted by the charitable bounty of well disposed Marchants) they ariued vpon the coast of England.

In all this Time his Father and Mother hearing no newes of him, Imagined him to be dead, which was such a griefe to his mother, that it brought her (as was imagined) before her time to her end.

On the other side he calling to minde, his stubborne carriage, and wilfull disobedience, was ashamed to be knowne for their Sonne : But altogether loathing his former courses, bound himselfe Prentice to a Barber Surgeon farre off in the West, with whome hauing serv'd most of his Time, and well profited in his profession, his Master sent him Surgeon in a Ship to the *Indyes*.

1 Original, *a day shore*.

Where such good liking was conceited of him, that after a voyage or two for his Maister, his Time expired, and some gratuitie receiued of his maister for his true and faithfull seruice, he went out againe for himselfe: Hauing thus wrought himselfe an Estate of some two hundred pound and better. Comming this last voyage from the *Indyes*, and longing as 'tis the nature of all men, at last to see and visit his Father, Countrey and acquaintance, from whome he had now for the space of fifteene yeares beene a stranger: and the Ship which he came in, staying in the Riuer being vnladen, and euery man honestly paide his wages and what he had in venter.

[Woodcut of Ship.]

A Ship being ready bound for *Cornwall*, he became a passenger in her, and no sooner put to Sea, but a gentle Calme vsherd the Ship, that seemed to dally and play the wanton on the curld bosome of the waues, a shoale of Porpisses that like actiue tumblers vauted [1] in their watry progresse, made them such varietie of present pastime, they seem'd secure and free from all danger that misfortune could any way threaten.

But note the euent: being within kenne of the English shore, a pitchie Cloud so darke and palpable, as day and night were indistinguishable, Inueloped the Sunne, vnto this the Windes like great men bowed to one another, Raine brauld lowde and talkt roughly : In this night of horror now was the ship banded like a Ball against the roughest heauen, and in the same instant throwne downe

1 Vaulted : original, *hauted.*

as low as the Center : billow cuffes billow, and one waue buffets another, so full of disordered rudeness grew the Elements, as the world seem'd nothing else but like an Image of the first generall Chaos. In conclusion, so grosse and palpable grew this confusion, as had not the tongue of eternity cried *fiat dies* a second time, it had beene eternall night. During this mutenous insurrection of the waues, The Maister being a Stranger, and vnacquainted with the coast, split his Ship against a Rocke ; at which, imagine in what a confused clamour they were : some praying, some cursing, and others exclayming, which would haue rent a mans heart harder then the rocke they ran against. But in vaine, the storme like a cruell tyrant hauing predestined all their ruines, spared neither young nor old, but made a generall massacreof them all:

This young Factour onely escapt : who with many other the terrible tempests in action,[1] cast divers plots for safety, and withall, as they were mindfull of their liues, so did they not altogether forget the means, and divers Jewels they had aboard ; especially our young English Factour, who well experienced in swimming, loaded himselfe with so much golde, as he thought might be no wayes preiudiciall to his life.

Thus loaden with Jewels and Gold, by the will of heaven, and his owne carefull and painefull industry, sometime swimming, and other whiles catching hold of rent plancks and the like: For the Ship once wrackt,

---

[1] Who, with many other, the terrible tempests being in action, cast divers plots?

the Sea grew calme, and the windes (like tyrants) hauing done what hauock they could, flew [playing ?] to the shore, and there sate smiling at the ruines they had made.

Our young Gallant a shore, wet, and vnacquainted by reason of his discontinuance, enquired of the next Passenger[1] he met the way to *Perin*, who accordingly directed him.

Being entred the Towne, he (without acquainting any man with his name or businesse) repaires to the house where some sixteene yeares since being an Inne, he had lefte his owne Father dwelling : where enquiring as a stranger for such a man, he heard that his first wife being dead, he had married a second, and given that house (being a well esteemed Inne) to the Maister of it, in way of dowrie with one of his daughters, being sister to this our distressed Travailler.

This woman he desired to see and conferre withall, who by reason of his long absence, had altogether forgot him : he notwithstanding asked if she neuer had a wilde Youth (concealing his owne name) to her Brother : She answered yes, and one that aboue all the rest her Father and Mother cockred and loued : But he was long since taken by the Turkes and died (as they were informed) a Gally slave: he laboured to perswade the contrary, and gaue many and certaine likelihoodes, that he was the same party : Telling the name of his Godfathers, and where they dwelt, as also with whom, and in what place he went to Schoole. But all to no purpose, so throughly

1 Passer-by.

was she grounded in the report of his death, as nothing could perswade the contrary.

Till at last she called to minde an infallible token, which was this, that if he were her brother, hee had a great red Moale growing in the bent of his left arme, by which, shee had often heard her Mother say, especially on her death bed, that if euer it were his fortune to come againe, they might easily know him amongst a thousand. And except he could shew her that, all other proofes in the world should never perswade her that he was her brother, but some cunning Impostore: whereupon, not willing to hold her longer in suspence, he opened his bosome, and gave her certaine testimony of the trueth.

At sight whereof shee fell about his necke and kissed him, not being able (for the violence of instant ioy) to refraine from shedding of teares. The young man demanded how his Father, Mother, and the rest of their kindred did : but when hee heard that his Mother was dead, and the chiefe cause of it proceeded from his disobedient stubbornnese and obstinate course, he fell into such Weeping, she had much labour to comfort him, requesting him to come in, and take such entertainement as her house could of the suddaine afford him.

To which he would in no wise consent, till had seene [1] done his duty too, and crau'd pardon of his Father, who dwelt at a Countrey house of his wives, some three or foure miles distant.

From which by many forceable reasons she labour'd

---

[1] Till he had seene?

to diswade him, *viz.* That their Mother in Law might haue no iust cause to hit their Father in the teeth with his Sonnes basenes, being poorely appareld, and newly Sea-wrackt, nor thinke he came for a stocke to set vp his Trade with, especially considering that by the marriages, and great portions giuen with his Children, his quiet life was much disturbed, and his estate more impoverisht : His answere was, that his comming should be a hindrance neither to her nor his Father: For though in that poore and thinne habit, he brought enough for himselfe, and if needs were, to be a helpe and supply to them, and the rest of their poore family.

Onely his request was, that shee would conceale his Name and comming, not onely from the houshold, but her Husband, to try if his Father (as she already had beene) could be deceived in his acquaintance, or not : And if he were, that then the next morning she would meete him there at Breakfast, with as many of their Kindred as was possible, because that besides his presence, hee had brought that home, that being seene and knowne, would make their Joy a great deale the more full : when the good olde man should not only finde of a stubberne and disobedient, a dutifull and penetent childe ; and not so onely, but one that by his painefull industry, got that in his youth, which should relieue and comfort his Father in his declining estate.

These premises considered, she condiscended to his request, and onely tasting a cup of Beere, for that time parted : He iourneying towards his Father, and she to meditate vpon the passionate Joy would befall their whole Family the next day at Breakfast. So leaue we them and speake a worde or two of the good olde man their Father.

Who by good House keeping, associating himselfe with Knights and Gentlemen somwhat aboue his estate : As also by preferring his owne, and his second wiues Kindred to great and wealthy marriages, had brought himselfe much behinde hand in the world. To all this his wife being somewhat churlish, and more respecting her owne future estate, then his present welfare : And as it is common with all Mothers, to preferre the good of their owne children before them, to whome they are but mothers in Law. All these thinges put together, but especially seeing his supposed friends, and auncient company keepers, begin to thinke and draw their neckes out of the collers as the Proverbe is, was no little griefe to the heart of the good olde man.

To this a friend gaue him notice, of an Execution of Three hundred pound come out against him : that much disquieted him : His Sonne comes to the woman, demaunding Lodging and meate, being a poore Sea fairing man, and theire ship and all their goods lost at Sea.

She answered, she would aske her husbands consent : which she did.

He intreated her of all loue she would vse him well, vrging he had a sonne at Sea himselfe (if aliue at least) and knew not what want he might stand in : She sayes he is a poore knaue : so much more neede of reliefe, answered her Husband : She rayles at him, and tels him such Prodigalitie hath brought him so low : And such Charity he hopes will be a meanes to raise him as high as euer he was : Sent for him in, gets him a warme Caudle, caused a Pullet to be kil'd, and such fare as his present estate afforded prouided he.

Supper being ended, the good olde man tho desirous of newes, (and rather if he could heare any of his Sonne) yet in regard of the young mans late sea-wracke, and sharpe travaile, hee put off their discourse till the next morning, and so taking leaue, betooke him to his bed, requesting his wife (for other seruants all that time were not in their house) to light the young man to his lodging.

The Olde man gone, his wife (as the custome of most Women is) desirous of newes, fell into a serious discourse with him, of meny, and (as the young man thought) frivol-ous matters : and imagining (perhaps iustly) that she feared he might in the night steale somewhat, or offer them be-ing lone people some discourtesie : To cleare all manner of suspect, he pluckt out divers baggs of Golde, to the value of some foure hundred pound, vsing these or the like words: Mrs. that you may know your kindnesses are not cast away vpon some base or vngratefull Peasant, ill nurtured in the rules of requitall, keepe this for me till to morrow: when before some good frinds of mine,

[Woodcut of group.]

which I purpose to send for, I will shew my selfe a will-ing and bountifull debter, and acquaint them and you with the discourse of my whole trauailes, which I make no doubt will be both pleasing and acceptable to all: with these or the like wordes, giuing her the golde to lay by till morning, she lighted him vp to bed, where we leaue him to his rest, and returne to the couetous Step-mother.

Who thinking of her present wants, and looking of the golde, cast about twenty wayes, how to inioy it for her owne, when presently the Deuill, that is alwayes ready to take hold of the least aduantage that may be to increase his Kingdome, whispered this comfort in her eare, shew-ing her the golden temptation: saying, all this will I giue thee, if thou wilt but make away a poore stranger that sleepes vnder thy mercy.

She like her first Grandam, seeing the golde faire to looke too, and the taske easily and without much danger to be affected, tooke the Deuill at his worde, and tyed herselfe to him with an oath, that if she might peaceably inioy the Gold, the true owner of it should neuer wake.

Here now were fit occasion to talke of Golde : the paine, labour and danger a man takes to compasse it, and the infinite vexations, troubles, and casualties a man vndergoes to keepe it : so that I may speake of gold, as the Macedon did of a Kingdome, it is more difficult to keepe then conquer : but of that at some other time and in fitter place : She resolued to keepe the gold, tho for it she looses her life, and forfeits her soule : For where the Deuill playes the Lawyer thats his ordinary fee.

First therefore, she goes vp to her husband, whome after she had wak'd, she questions how and what course he will take to auoyde the Execution come out against him : He requests her to be quiet, and that it was now no fit time of night to dispute of such businesse : If the worst came that could, he had [1] friends and Children would not see him sinke vnder so sleight a burthen.

She answered, trusting to friends and relying vpon children, (into whose hands he had put his whole estate) had brought them so much behinde hand as they were. Telling him that if he would be rul'd by her, he should rid himselfe of all debt and danger, without helpe either of friends or children: to whom, whosoever trusteth shall finde that he leanes on a broken staffe, or a shiuered reede: he requests to know how: She tels him by meanes of the poore Saylor that lodged there acquainting him with what store of Golde he had about him, and how easily without danger (comming in late and vnseene the same night) they might make it all theirs.

He seeing her thoughts set all on murther, mildely diswaded her, laying before her the ineuetable dangers, and strange Judgements of God, show'd vpon people in the like kinde of offending : But when all that preuail'd not, he concluded his speech with that part of Scripture: *What will it auayle a man or a woman to get the whole world, and loose his owne soule,* and so settled himselfe to sleepe.

But all in vaine, for such deepe Impression of gaine, and palpable reasons of safety, had the Deuill granted [2] in her thoughts, 't was impossible to rub them out : and therefore in stead of desisting from her tended practise, she began to make it good, and shew deuilish arguments

1 Original, *have.*   2 grafted ?

to approue the lawfulnes of it : Insomuch, that to conclude her deuilish perswasions, drew the good olde man
out of his bed, with an intent to doe a murther, which,
murther it selfe would haue blusht to haue committed :
Twice by her deuillish inticements did he attempt it, and
twice his better Genius counseld him to the contrary.
At last, the Deuill, for the more valiantly he is resisted
growes the more malicious: by whose perswasion, the
olde man the second time in bed, hauing biterly denyed
the bloody act, and given her and the Deuill (whose ad-
uocate she was) theire answere as hee well hopt : she
comes the third time to his bed side, and to make her
temptation the more forcible, poures out the gold, fetch-
ing her hellish arguments *a minore ad maius*, thus : how
easily and with what little or no danger such a huge masse
of wealth might be purchased : which when he refeld by
vrging the vnlawfulnesse of it, she burst out into bitter
[execrations ?] and cursings, calling him faint hearted
coward, and wished, that if he did let slip that occasion,
hee might lye and rot in a Gaole, vowing that she would
not onely animate and set on all his Creditors to his bitter vndoing but dishearten and drawe all her and his
friends from helping and releeving him.

In conclusion, the Diuell and she prevailed, and on
hee goes the third time to attempt this deede of dark-
nesse, and entred the chamber, so deadly was her intent,
she thrust the knife in his hand, and stood hartning of him
on at the dore : he comming to the bed side, found him
fast a sleepe, and looking stedfastly vpon him, a drop of
blood fell from his nose vpon the young mans breast, and

seemed to blush and looke red, as if it had in dumbe
signe disswaded him from that diuellish intent. To conclude the bloodie deede is done, an innocent sonne slaine
by a guilty Father: his life blood shed by him from
whom both life and blood were received. A cruell
Murther, and so vnnaturall, as time hath not in all his
Recordes one more horrid and detestable : to see what a
pitteous groane and ruthfull looke the dying sonne cast
vpon the murtherous Father. I leaue to their considerations, that either knew the loue of a father to a sonne,
or a sonne to the father : onely this one note worthy remembrance I here credibly recite, that iust as the knife
was entering his throat, the screech-owle beat her pineons
against the window, and gaue a fearefull shrieke at the
beds head, as if she had said Awake young man awake,
but all in vaine, the Innocent is dead, and the guilty pos-
sest his gold.

The next morning very early, the sister according to
promise lights at the gate, and after her duty done to her
Father, desires to see and speake with her brother: the
old man amazed at this kind of visitation, askes what
brother she meant: she replies: the young man that in the
habite of a poore Saylor came the last night, to demaund
lodging, promised as that morning to meete her and
diuers other of their kindred, which she had brought to
Breakefast, and that he had brought home store of gold,
with which he purposed to pay his Fathers debts. The
olde man hearing this discourse, betwixt feare and hor-
rour, looked pale and trembled, yet seeing no remedy,
hee demaunded how she knew that young man to be her

brother: after many other probable likelihoods, she naimed the moale in the bent of his left arme: at hearing of which, without further wordes, as if he had beene strucke with a sodaine extasie: he runnes vp to the Chamber where this hainous murther was committed, and finding the token true, with the same knife he had kild his Sonne, he murthered himselfe: his Wife seeing her Husband stay somewhat longer then she expected, runnes vp after him to see the event, where finding her husband dead in his Sonnes armes, the Deuill on one side, and her owne guilty conscience on the other, telling and vrging her to be the cause of all this: her conscience perswading she had deserued death of body in this world; and the Deuill assuring her, she could not escape damnation in the world to come, Tooke the same knife (yet reeking with the blood of her breathlesse husband) and with it ript vp her owne bosome: the Daughter staying below, wondering neither Father, Brother nor Mother came downe (great with childe as she was) went by the staires: where she became a witnesse to the most lamentable (and worthiest to be pittied) Spectacle that ever eye saw.

The couetous Step-mother not yet altogether dead, as well as she could in broken accents excused her husband, and acknowledged

[Woodcut of the scene
printed as frontispiece to this volume.]

her selfe the ground & Author of all this: which hindred the good woman from doing instant violence vpon herselfe: but such was her extreame griefe, to see a Father murther his owne Sonne first, then himselfe, and a couetous step-Mother author of all this: she grew franticke, and threw herselfe first into the Armes of her Father, then of her Brother, kissing the one, and showring teares vpon the other, with such ardor of affection and violence of passion, it made all the standers by with a generall voyce cry out: It was the Bloodiest and most Inhuman murther, the Countrey was euer guilty of.

And so to the end it may be a warning, to all couetous ste⎡ -Mothers and a content for all easie Fathers to auoyde the like hereafter: At the entreaty of diuers Gentlemen in the Countrey, It is as neare the life as Pen and Incke could draw it out, thus put in Print.

FINIS

[Woodcut: arabesque]

———————

For comparison the condensed version of Frankland is added, as it is given in the *Postscript* to George Colman's edition of the play in 1783.

II

The miserable condition of sinful man in sundry examples of these present and of former times, should mind us hourly to beg of God preventing grace, lest we fall into temptations of sin and Satan ; such have been the calamities of ages past, at present are, and will be to come ; histories of *theft*, *rapine*, *murther*, and such like.

One of wondrous note happened at Perinin in Cornwall, in September, a bloody and unexampled murther, by a father and mother upon their own son, and then upon themselves.

He had been blessed with ample possessions, and fruitful issue, unhappy only in a younger son ; who taking liberty from his father's bounty, and with a crew of like condition, that were wearied on land, they went roving to sea ; and in a small vessel southward, took booty, from all whom they could master, and so increasing force and wealth, ventured on a Turk's-man in the Streights ; but by mischance their own powder fired themselves ; and our gallant, trusting to his skilful swimming, got ashore upon Rhodes, with the best of his jewels about him, where, offering some to sale to a Jew, who knew them to be the governor's of Algier, he was apprehended, and as a pyrate sentenced to the gallies amongst other christians, whose miserable slavery made them all studious of freedom ; and with wit and valour took opportunity and means to murther some officers, got aboard of an English ship, and came safe to London, where his Majesty and some skill made him servant to a chyrurgion, and sudden preferment to the East Indies ; there by this means he got mony, with which returning back, he designed himself for his native county Cornwall ; and in a small ship from London, sailing to the West, was cast away upon the coast ; but his excellent skill in swimming, and former fate to boot, brought him safe to shore ; where since his fifteen years absence, his father's former fortunes much decayed, now retired him not far off to a country habitation, in debt and danger.

His sister, he finds married to a mercer, a meaner match than her birth promised; to her at first appears a poor stranger, but in private reveals himself, and withal what jewels and gold he had concealed in a bow-case [1] about him; and concluded that the next day he intended to appear to his parents, and to keep his disguise till she and her husband should meet, and make their common joy compleat.

Being come to his parents, his humble behaviour, suitable to his suit of cloaths, melted the old couple to so much compassion, as to give him covering from the cold season under their outward roof; and by degrees his travelling tales told with passion to the aged people, made him their guest, so long by the kitchen fire, that the husband took leave and went to bed, and soon after his true stories working compassion in the weaker vessel, she wept, and so did he; but compassionate of her tears, he comforted her with a piece of gold, which gave assurance that he deserved a lodging, to which she brought him, and being in bed shewed her his girdled wealth, which he said was sufficient to relieve her husband's wants, to spare for himself; and being very weary, fell fast asleep.

The wife tempted with the golden bait of what she had, and eager of enjoying all, awaked her husband with this news, and her contrivance what to do; and though with horrid apprehension he oft refused, yet her puling fondness (Eve's inchantments) moved him to consent,

---

[1] This must mean a bent case, tied round the body. See below ' his girdled wealth.' (Cf. bow-window = semicircular window.)

and rise to be master of all ; and both of them to murder
the man, which instantly they did, covering the corps
under the cloaths till opportunity to convey it out of the
way.

The early morning hastens the sister to her father's
house, where she with signs of joy, enquires for a saylor
that should lodge there the last night ; the parents slightly
denied to have seen any such, until she told them that it
was her brother, her lost brother, by that assured scar
upon his arm cut with a sword in his youth, she knew
him ; and were all resolved this morning to meet there
and be merry.

The father hastily runs up, finds the mark, and with
horrid regret of this monstrous murther of his own son,
with the same knife cut his own throat.

The wife went up to consult with him, where in a
most strange manner beholding them both in blood, wild
and aghast, with the instrument at hand, readily rips up
her own belly till the guts tumbled out.

The daughter, doubting the delay of their absence,
searches for them all, whom she found out too soon, with
the sad sight of this scene ; and being overcome with
horror and amaze of this deluge of destruction, she sank
down and died, the fatal end of that family.

The truth of which was frequently known, and flew to
court in this guise ; but the imprinted relation conceals
their names, in favour to some neighbour of repute and
a-kin to that family.

The same sense makes me silent also.

𝔅𝔦𝔟𝔩𝔦𝔬𝔤𝔯𝔞𝔭𝔥𝔶

The place of publication is London unless otherwise noted.

I. TEXTS

This list includes separate editions, adaptations, and translations, besides issues in collective editions of Lillo's plays, and with those of other dramatists.

A. THE LONDON MERCHANT, OR GEORGE BARNWELL

1731. 8vo. THE LONDON MERCHANT : OR THE HISTORY OF GEORGE BARNWELL. First and second editions. 1st and 2d, Brit. Mus. ; 1st, Harv. Coll. Lib.

1732. 8vo. THE LONDON MERCHANT : OR THE HISTORY OF GEORGE BARNWELL. Fourth edition. Yale Univ. Lib.

1740. 8vo. THE LONDON MERCHANT : OR THE HISTORY OF GEORGE BARNWELL. Seventh edition. Boston Pub. Lib., Harv. Coll. Lib.

1740. 8vo. THE WORKS OF THE LATE MR. GEORGE LILLO. John Gray.

1750 [?]. 12mo. THE WORKS OF THE LATE MR. GEORGE LILLO.

1762. 12mo. THE WORKS OF THE LATE MR. GEORGE LILLO.

1768. 12mo. THE WORKS OF THE LATE MR. GEORGE LILLO. Edinburgh.

1770. 12mo. THE LONDON MERCHANT : OR THE HISTORY OF GEORGE BARNWELL. Printed for T. Lowndes, T. Caslon, W. Nicoll, and S. Bladon.

1772. 8vo. DER KAUFMANN VON LONDON, ODER BEGEBENHEITEN G. BARNWELLS. Ein bürgerliches Trauerspiel. Aus dem Englischen des Herrn Tillo übersetzt durch H. A. B. Neue Auflage. Hamburg.

1774. 12mo. THE WORKS OF THE LATE MR. GEORGE LILLO. Edinburgh.

1775. 8vo. THE WORKS OF MR. GEORGE LILLO, WITH SOME ACCOUNT OF HIS LIFE [by T. Davies]. 2 vols. T. Davies. Second edition, 1810.

1775. 8vo. DE KOOPMAN VAN LONDON. Burgerlyk treurspel ... naar het Engelsche van den Heer Tillo. Spectatoriaale Schouwburg. Part VIII. Amsterdam.

1775. 8vo. LE MARCHAND DE LONDRES, OU L'HISTOIRE DE GEORGE BARNWELL. Tragédie bourgeoise traduite de l'Anglois de M. Lillo [by P. Clément]. Seconde édition, augmentée de deux scènes. Londres.

1776. 12mo. THE LONDON MERCHANT: OR THE HISTORY OF GEORGE BARNWELL. Bell's *British Theatre*, vol. v.

1776. THE LONDON MERCHANT: OR THE HISTORY OF GEORGE BARNWELL. *The Tragic Theatre*, vol. VII.

1776. 8vo. THE LONDON MERCHANT: OR THE HISTORY OF GEORGE BARNWELL. *The New English Theatre*, vol. VI.

1776. 12mo. THE LONDON MERCHANT: OR THE HISTORY OF GEORGE BARNWELL. Marked with the Variations in the Manager's Book at the Theatre Royal in Drury Lane. Printed for T. Lowndes, T. Caslon, W. Nicoll, T. Davies, and S. Bladon.

1777. 8vo. GEORGE BARNWELL: a tragedy. J. Wenman.

1777. 12mo. GEORGE BARNWELL: a tragedy. W. Oxlade.

1781. 8vo. DER KAUFMANN VON LONDON, ODER BEGEBENHEITEN G. BARNWELLS. Neue Auflage. Hamburg.

1793. 12mo. GEORGE BARNWELL: a tragedy. Belknap & Hall, Boston, Mass.

1794. 12mo. GEORGE BARNWELL: a tragedy. Third edition, Worcester, Mass.

1797. 8vo. GEORGE BARNWELL: a tragedy. Bell's *British Theatre*, vol. XIV.

1807 [?]. 12mo. GEORGE BARNWELL: a tragedy. With remarks by Mrs. Inchbald.

1811. 8vo. GEORGE BARNWELL: a tragedy. *The Modern British Drama*, vol. II.

1814. 16mo. THE LONDON MERCHANT, OR, THE HISTORY OF GEORGE BARNWELL. [Dibdin's] *The London Theatre*, vol. IX.

1816. 12mo. GEORGE BARNWELL. [Mrs. Inchbald's] *The British Theatre*, vol. XI.

1823. 8vo. GEORGE BARNWELL. [W. H. Oxberry's] *The New English Drama*, vol. XVII.

1824. 16mo. GEORGE BARNWELL [with three other plays]. *Living Plays*. New York.

1826. 16mo. GEORGE BARNWELL. With a wood engraving. Cumberland's *British Theatre*.

1832. GEORGE BARNWELL. *The British Drama*. Vol. II. Also 1864, and Phila. 1853.

1846. GEORGE BARNWELL. *Modern Standard Drama*, vol. XI. N. Y.

1864. 8vo. GEORGE BARNWELL. Illustrated. *The British Drama*, vol. II.

18—. 12mo. GEORGE BARNWELL. French's *Standard Drama*, no. 88.

1868. 12mo. GEORGE BARNWELL. Lacy's *Acting Edition of Plays*, vol. LXXIX.

There are also undated editions of the eighteenth century, "Printed for and sold by the Booksellers in Town and Country."

B. FATAL CURIOSITY

1737. 8vo. FATAL CURIOSITY: a true tragedy of three acts. As it is acted at the New Theatre in the Hay-Market. Brit. Mus., Bost. Pub. Lib., Yale Univ. Lib.

1740. 8vo. THE WORKS OF THE LATE MR. GEORGE LILLO. John Gray.

1775. 8vo. THE WORKS OF MR. GEORGE LILLO, WITH SOME ACCOUNT OF HIS LIFE [by T. Davies]. 2 vols. T. Davies. Vol. II. Second edition, 1810.

1780. 8vo. THE WORKS OF MR. GEORGE LILLO.

1783. 8vo. FATAL CURIOSITY: a true tragedy. With alterations [and a Postscript, by G. Colman].

1784. 8vo. THE FATAL CURIOSITY: a true tragedy. With a short account of the author's life and an explanatory index [in German]. Nordhausen.

1784. 8vo. THE SHIPWRECK, OR FATAL CURIOSITY. A tragedy

altered from Lillo [by H. Mackenzie]. As performed at the Theatre Royal in Covent Garden. T. Cadell.

[**1785.**] 8vo. STOLZ UND VERZWEIFLUNG. Schauspiel in drey Acten nach Lillo. [By W. H. Brömel.] Brömel's *Beitrag zur Deutschen Bühne.* [Dessau and Leipzig.]

1791. 8vo. STOLZ UND VERZWEIFLUNG. *Deutsche Schaubühne,* vol. XXI. Augsburg.

1796. 8vo. FATAL CURIOSITY. Bell's *British Theatre,* vol. XXIII.

1800. PRESERVATION; OR THE HOVEL OF THE ROCKS : a play, in five acts : interspersed with part of Lillo's drama, in three acts, called "Fatal Curiosity." Cox, Charleston. Bost. Pub. Lib.

1808. 12mo. FATAL CURIOSITY. [Mrs. Inchbald's] *The British Theatre,* vol. XI.

1811. 8vo. FATAL CURIOSITY. *The Modern British Drama,* vol. II.

1817. 12mo. FATAL CURIOSITY. With remarks by Mrs. Inchbald.

1824. 8vo. FATAL CURIOSITY. *The British Drama,* vol. I.
1826. 8vo. FATAL CURIOSITY. *The London Stage,* vol. III.
1832. 8vo. FATAL CURIOSITY. Illustrated. *The British Drama,* vol. I. Also 1864, and Phila. 1853.

II. WORKS BIOGRAPHICAL AND CRITICAL

(*See also the memoirs and critical material prefixed to the Texts enumerated under I, and notes to Introductions.*)

1747. LIST OF ALL THE ENGLISH DRAMATIC POETS. Printed with T. Whincop's *Scanderbeg ;* p. 258.

1753. LIVES OF THE POETS OF GREAT BRITAIN AND IRELAND. By Mr. [Theophilus] Cibber, and other Hands. Vol. v, pp. 338–340 : *Mr. George Lillo.*

1781. PHILOLOGICAL INQUIRIES ; in three Parts. James Harris. Parts I and II, pp. 154–158 ; 169–172.

1798. 12mo. BARNWELL. A novel. By T. S. Surr. Fourth edition, 1807.

1800. A Complete History of the Stage. C. Dibdin. Vol. v. pp. 61–64.

1810. 12mo. Memoirs of George Barnwell; the unhappy subject of Lillo's celebrated tragedy. By a descendant of the Barnwell family. Harlow.

1812. Biographia Dramatica. D. E. Baker. Continued by D. Reed and S. Jones. Vol. i, part ii, pp. 453–455, and vol. ii, pp. 224–227 and 370–378.

1832. Some Account of the English Stage. [Genest, J.] Vols. iii–viii *passim*, and *Index* in vol. x. Bath.

1857. Ueber den Stoff von Z. Werner's Vierundzwanzigsten Februar. R. Köhler. (Weimarer Sonntagsblatt. Repr. in vol. iii of Kleinere Schriften, herausg. v. J. Botte. Berlin. 1900. pp. 185–199.

1858. Gesammelte Werke. G. E. Lessing. Vol. iv : *Vorreden zu Diderots Theater*; vol. vii : *Hamburgische Dramaturgie*. Leipzig.

1865. Geschichte der Englischen Literatur, etc. H. Hettner. (*Literaturgesch. d. achtzehnten Jahrh.*, part i.) Especially pp. 514–522. Brunswick.

1866. Diderot als Dichter und Dramaturg. J. C. F. Rosenkranz (*Diderot's Leben und Werke*, vol. i, pp. 267–316). Leipzig.

1869. Lessing and Swift. Caro. Jena.

1874-75. Œuvres. D. Diderot. Vols. vii–viii (*Belles-Lettres*, vols. iv–v). Paris : Garnier Frères. [For references see *Introduction* to this volume, p. xxxvii.]

1877. Hamburgische Dramaturgie. G. E. Lessing. Erläutert von F. Schröter u. R. Theile, Esp. pp. 489–520. Halle.

1882. The Story of Fatal Curiosity. W. E. A. Axon. Notes and Queries. 6th series. Vol. v, pp. 21–23.

1883 [?]. Das Schicksalsdrama (*Deutsche National-Literatur*, vol. 151). J. Minor. Berlin and Stuttgart.

1883. Die Schicksalstragödie in ihren Hauptvertretern. J. Minor. Frankfort.

1888. George Lillo. E. W. L. Hoffmann. Inaugural Dissertation. Marburg.

1890. Zu Lillo's Kaufmann von London. A. Brandl. *Vierteljahrschrift für litteraturgeschichte*, III, 47–62.

1893. Dictionary of National Biography, vol. XXIII, pp. 252–255, *Lillo, George*. By A. W. Ward.

1904. English Literature and Society in the Eighteenth Century. Sir L. Stephen. (*Ford Lectures*, 1903,) pp. 164–166.

R